RETURN TO THE TOP

The Inside Story of Carolina's 1993 NCAA Championship

HUGH MORTON

Foreword by Dean Smith
Featuring the work of the following Tar Heel alumni:
Exclusive diaries by seniors Scott Cherry, George Lynch,
Henrik Rödl, Travis Stephenson and Matt Wenstrom;
words and photos from Rick Brewer, Art Chansky, Bob Donnan,
Woody Durham, Dave Glenn, Ron Green Jr., Alfred Hamilton Jr.,
Larry Keith, Hugh Morton, Lee Pace and Mark Whicker.

With 64,151 watching in person and millions more viewing from home, Donald Williams held the last point of the college basketball season in his hands (previous page). Pretending he was alone in a gym, Williams swished the final four points to secure Carolina's 77-71 win over Michigan and set Franklin Street afire with celebration (overleaf).

With Appreciation
To Corporate Sponsors:

Alexander Julian, Inc.
The Burris Agency
Champion Products
Converse
East-West Partners
The Hickory Printing Group
Landfall
Jefferson-Pilot
Willis Corroon

RETURN TO THE TOP

The Inside Story of Carolina's 1993 NCAA Championship

Publisher	Art Chansky
Editor/Designer	Lee Pace
Associate Editor	Jim Wilson
Chief Photographers	Hugh Morton, Bob Donnan

Published by Village Sports, Inc.
in association with
The UNC Department of Athletics and General Alumni Association.

Special Thanks To:

Linda Belans, Jim Bounds, Elvis Brathwaite, Rick Brewer, Scott Cherry, Andrew Cline, Sherry Clontz, Roger Cohen, Doug Dibbert, Mike Dickson, Mark Dolejs, Leslie Drinkwalter, Jean Durham, Woody Durham, Jeff Elliott, Phil Ford, Dave Glenn, Jerry Green, Ron Green Jr., John Grimes, Bill Guthridge, Alfred Hamilton Jr., Dave Hanners, Jim Heavner, Hurley the dog, Larry Keith, Ruth Kirkendall, Leslie Kovach, Angela Lee, George Lynch, Paul MaGann, Scott Montross, Mick Mixon, Will Owens, Catherine Pace & the girls, Millie Pridgen, Jack Reece, Henrik Rödl, Scott Sharpe, Gray Shields, Dean Smith, Lee Snyder, Travis Stephenson, Susan Strobel, John Swofford, Bernard Thomas, Kay Thomas, Matt Wenstrom, Karen Wertman, Mark Whicker, Bill Whitley, Randy Wiel, Betsy Wilson, Dot Wilson, Bob Woodruff, Kaelin Woods, Linda Woods.

Library of Congress Catalog Card Number: 93-60554
ISBN: 1-880123-07-X

Front end sheet photo by Scott Sharpe/The News & Observer; Back end sheet photo by Hugh Morton.

Derrick Phelps was a cornerstone to Carolina's success with his floor leadership and defense.

MARK DOLEJS/THE HERALD-SUN

Tar Heels, Dean Smith all smiles as Duke AD Tom Butters, chairman of the NCAA Men's Basketball Committee, presents the No. 1 trophy.

SUPERDOME WELCOMES
NO. CAROLINA TARHEELS

CONTENTS

0   0   50:49

HUGH MORTON

Brian Reese's explosiveness and emotional play helped pull the Tar Heels through several close calls.

1993 Team Special, Even By Heels' Lofty Standard.

Carolina basketball fans, and I count myself among them, took to the 1993 Tar Heels right away. We all sensed early that this team had a chance to do something very special, even by Carolina standards.

It may have been how hard they played, or their dogged attitude toward winning. Watching them on and off the court, I was struck by their chemistry and togetherness.

Being around them some at games and on the road, I noticed how much they seemed to like and respect each other. They had a certain comfort level, beyond the norm. That was sure the case when Pat Sullivan was comfortable enough to remind the President of the United States that we had "waxed" his Arkansas team in the regional!

This Carolina team had a personality right from the beginning of the season. And the fans loved the obvious enthusiasm with which they played.

I thought that was demonstrated by that little incident in New Orleans, when George Lynch and Eric Montross, in the heat of competition, had a mild disagreement on the court. Then, minutes later, they were walking arm-in-arm with big smiles on their faces.

George is certainly one of the greatest players to ever wear a Carolina uniform. A lot of us knew it from his freshman year, but it seems like all of a sudden this season people said, "Hey, this guy's been doing these things every game for four years, and it's about time we appreciated him."

George finally got all of the honors he deserved.

Equally appropriate was Coach Smith winning his second national championship. He has given more to college basketball than anyone else, and he so richly deserves to be honored by the way success has become defined.

I enrolled as a student at Carolina in the fall of 1967, and Coach Smith had already been to the Final Four once. That was his first great push, when he won three straight Atlantic Coast Conference championships and reached the Final Four each year.

So, as an athletic director, I burst with pride and appreciation for the kind of basketball program we have here at Carolina. Things are done the right way, and I can sleep at night not having to worry about the integrity or its commitment to academics.

On the national level, the basketball program has so much to do with how our whole athletic department and institution are perceived. Carolina basketball is about winning, but it's also about total winning.

Quality in every respect.

I join all of you in saluting the 1993 national champions, a team that made every Carolina fan even prouder than usual to be a Tar Heel.

John D. Swofford
Director of Athletics

To the Tar Heels:
No. 1 in 1992-93,
No. 1 forever.

Front row: Strength Coach Harley Dartt, Trainer Marc Davis, Head Coach Dean Smith, Travis Stephenson, Henrik Rödl, Matt Wenstrom, George Lynch, Scott Cherry, Assistant Coach Phil Ford, Assistant to the Athletic Director Dave Hanners, Assistant Coach Bill Guthridge. Back row: Head Manager Sam Rogers, Manager Bobby Dawson, Manager Laura Johnson, Larry Davis, Derrick Phelps, Pat Sullivan, Ed Geth, Eric Montross, Serge Zwikker, Kevin Salvadori, Brian Reese, Dante Calabria, Donald Williams, Manager Chuck Lisenbee, Manager Eddie Wills, Manager Eran Bloxam. Not pictured: Assistant Coach Randy Wiel.

Another Season For The Books.

We are excited to have had such an enjoyable year, one filled with so many memorable moments. Our players challenged themselves from the off-season on to be the best they could be, and they accomplished their ultimate goal.

Only one team in the NCAA Tournament can finish the season with a victory, and I'm so happy for our seniors that they did it in their last chance. The coaches have a chance every year, but the players only have four shots at it. The balance of talent in college basketball today makes the odds overwhelming, so our players can take tremendous pride in what they achieved.

Like all of our Carolina teams, this one played hard, played together and made most of the big plays; we also had the good fortune to avoid injuries to key players and had the bounce of the ball go our way on some occasions. I've always said you have to be both good and lucky, and we were.

I do know we couldn't have accomplished any of our goals without the seniors. I don't see how we can improve on our senior leadership next season, which is a real challenge for Kevin, Brian, Derrick, Eric and Pat.

Our seniors all earned their degrees in May and will go on to be successful, whether they play basketball or not. Preparing themselves for the rest of their lives is the most important objective, and it's nice to win some basketball games along the way.

George Lynch has been a special player and a real joy to have coached in college. Whoever coaches him in professional basketball will be very lucky. He does everything, seems to be everywhere.

Coach Guthridge predicts that, next year, we'll be watching tape and wondering why we aren't getting as many loose balls. It will be because George isn't playing.

I don't like to compare players so I'll just say he's among the best offensive rebounders we've ever had, and certainly his effort was among the best. That means he's among the best offensive rebounders to ever play college basketball. His statistics over four years are just amazing but don't tell *all* the story.

Henrik Rödl is one of the smartest players I've had the privilege to be around. He was the most underrated player on the team, a great passer and defender. He's a very special young man who added so much to our team. Henrik will go on to play pro basketball in Germany, and then maybe he and Susan will come back to visit us, or he may choose to enter medical school here in Chapel Hill.

Our depth was such a big key this season, not in games as much as in practice. For someone who came in so highly recruited, Matt Wenstrom *chose* to have a great attitude every day he went out to practice or play. And that helped Eric and Kevin get ready. They really had some battles in practice.

And Matt was surely ready when called upon. I

HUGH MORTON

know one thing: We couldn't have won the Florida State game in Chapel Hill without Matt's help in the first half. Without him, we would have been too far behind. Matt will play basketball professionally and I believe will have an excellent career.

Someone else who could have gone to another school and played more is Scott Cherry. He was so valuable to us in practice, because he knew what we wanted and he can execute playing several positions. He should have played a lot more, except that we had three guards, Derrick Phelps, Henrik Rödl and Donald Williams, for the two guard positions. When one was hurt, Scott received more playing time.

Travis Stephenson continued our tradition of walk-ons earning a scholarship after they play on the junior varsity. We've always believed in a jayvee team, for the student body, and Travis proved that players who aren't recruited can certainly help the varsity.

I'm especially glad the seniors got a chance to write the diaries in this book. They've been such a special part of the program, and now they're getting to talk about it in their own words.

I'm looking forward to reading what each has to say!

Dean Smith

SENIOR
SCRAPBOOK

When Travis Stephenson, George Lynch, Scott Cherry, Henrik Rödl and Matt Wenstrom (L-R) gathered in the Smith Center in September to be photographed for the cover the Tar Heel media guide, their goal was to end the season with a New Orleans celebration. On the following 44 pages is the seniors' chronicle of how that dream came true.

TAR HEEL SENIORS, PRESEASON 1992-93

Stephenson rejoices with Serge Zwikker in last minute of NCAA title game.

MARK DOLEJS/
THE HERALD-SUN

Mid-Summer Night's Dream No Fish Story.

B Y T R A V I S S T E P H E N S O N

The record will forever show Carolina won the NCAA championship on that magical night in April in New Orleans. But for 11 of us, the road to the national title started the night in Lexington, Ky., a year earlier when Ohio State bounced us out of the 1992 Mideast Regional.

Some losses are more difficult to take than others. When you get soundly beaten by someone, like we did at Wake Forest earlier this year, all you can say is, "Good game," and go on to the next one. But when

Please turn to Page 18

Are we there yet?

BOB DONNAN

Lots of running, weight-lifting and practice during the hot summer months gave the Tar Heels plenty to celebrate during the basketball season.

you feel like you could have won, should have won, were in control to win a game—and then it slips away, you have to choke it down like a soggy piece of pizza. Ohio State was like that.

We had a five-point lead at halftime in that game and would have been further ahead had we not committed 12 turnovers. Jim Jackson and Lawrence Funderburke played great games, and they had a guy named Jamie Skelton come off the bench and light it up. We had two layups roll off the rim late in the game when we could have regained the lead, but we just could never get over the hump. They won, 80-73, and we were a very frustrated group.

I think something of an unspoken alliance was forged that night and it grew in the days that followed. We knew we couldn't accept losing like that. We knew we had lots of talent. The media and a lot of fans were ragging on Coach Smith and the team. We heard it over and over and over: "You guys can win 20 games, go to the Sweet 16 every year, but you can't win the big game." We got tired of that.

Then we had to watch Duke win another national championship. I don't want to take anything from them—they have a great program—but face it: They're eight miles away. All spring it was Duke this and Duke that. A lot of their guys come over here to party. We're only human; you see them come to your campus to socialize and it gets under your skin.

Then Coach Smith said something at the team's awards banquet that I think got our attention. He said he was "for real" when practice started in the fall, that we'd better come ready to play, ready to attack the year head-on. Nobody thought he was joking.

All these things combined to give us a tremendous resolve over the summer and early fall. Most everyone on the team was in summer school for at least one session.

Eric Montross and I moved into an apartment off-campus at the beginning of summer school, which Coach Smith allows players to do after their sophomore year. Eric and I became good friends at the beginning of the 1991-92 school year. I had just moved onto the basketball hall at Granville Towers after being invited by Coach Guthridge to try out for the varsity. After first coming to Carolina in the fall of 1988 with the idea of walking on the football team and running track, I'd gravitated to basketball and wound up playing JV basketball for Coach Wiel.

Eric and I shared a common bond of country music and the outdoors. One of my first days in Granville, I heard Alabama blaring from Eric's room. I thought he was just trying to razz the other guys, because rap was pretty dominant up there. But I went in his room and he had a long stack of country CDs. We talked about two hours straight about music, fishing, biking, skeet shooting, stuff like that. We've been good friends ever since.

We've taken a lot of abuse over our country music. Once we were in a steakhouse in Atlanta, where they had sawdust on the floors and played country music on the jukebox. This song came on, "Here's a Quarter, Call Someone Who Cares," and Coach Ford went crazy over that song. From then on, that became a running joke with Coach Ford. You might walk past him and he'd flip a quarter at you and say, "Call someone who cares."

My cousin, Mitchell Dixon, lives alongside a 40-acre lake on the other side of Raleigh. Eric and I would drive over there in the evenings a lot last summer, jump into a little battery powered boat and ride out onto the lake. We'd drop our lines into the water, fish for bass and enjoy the serenity and the quiet time to think.

I remember many of our conversations went along these lines:

"Man, all you've got to do is get into the NCAA Tournament and win six straight.

"Six good games and a little luck and you're the national champions.

"We've got as much chance as anyone.

"Four starters returning ... Henrik Rödl and Donald Williams to take Hubert Davis's spot. We've got as much talent as anyone.

"This is my last year, Eric. You're halfway out of here already.

"Where is it this year, New Orleans?"

Everyone on the team had his own way of channeling that dream of winning the Final Four in New Orleans, and that dream was embodied in the time we spent playing ball at the gym, running and lifting weights.

When we weren't involved in pick-up games, Eric and I would go off to one of the side goals and work together on individual moves. Eric's two priorities were to improve his hook shot and drop-step jumper. Coach Smith always talked about developing a favorite move and a counter. For Eric, that was the hook. Then he could play off that with a fake and quick drop-step. I'd feed him pass after pass after pass and he'd shoot. The hook shot was really a key for him this year. You get a 7-footer like Eric spreading out to shoot a hook, and you've got a lot of man to get through to get to the ball.

I was going to move from the four-spot (big forward) to three-spot (small forward) to back up Brian Reese and Pat Sullivan, so my priority was to improve my jumpshot. After Eric would work on hooks and drop-steps, I'd go out and shoot jumpers and he'd rebound. That's not to say my jumpshot was as important as Eric's hook, but that's the way our team was. It didn't matter if you were a starter or a walk-on—you were a part of the team, like everyone else.

All the other guys were working on various parts of their games, as well.

Derrick Phelps is always a force on defense, whether you're in a pick-up game or in the season. He'd just as soon pick your pocket in the summer as he would to go to the Final Four.

Brian Reese spent a lot of time last summer trying to cut down on his traveling calls. He's so quick and his speed is so explosive, the coaches wanted him to concentrate on getting the ball on the floor when he made that quick

move. As the season progressed, you could see that emphasis paid off.

I'll always remember all the time George Lynch spent in the weight room. George's game was the power game, the muscling-up inside, battling for rebounds. He loved the weight room. A lot of those rebounds George got during the season were paid for in the weight room during the summers.

The player we noticed the most over the summer was Donald Williams. His freshman year had been very difficult. I'd seen Donald

Stephenson's Career Walk-On Wild Side.

What better way to end your college career than to sink a running jumper at the buzzer against Duke in your final home game?

"It's not like we needed to score, but the guys on the bench were screaming for me to shoot," says Travis Stephenson. "It was a little flat—it was either going to go in or miss by a mile. When it went in, all I could do was laugh. Then the guys mobbed me.

"It was kind of special. It was like a flood of emotion came over us. We won our last home game, all the seniors started, Scott Cherry scored the first basket and I scored the last."

Stephenson's bucket capped the Tar Heels' 83-69 win and sent five seniors out in appropriate fashion after four years in the Smith Center.

Stephenson spent two years with the Tar Heel varsity after playing JV ball. He was originally a walk-on on the Carolina football team and a member of the track and field squad. A native of Clayton, Stephenson graduated this May with a degree in political science.

His post-graduate options include the possibility of becoming a coach, playing professional basketball in Europe or using his degree to seek a Congressional staff position.

play in high school, and there was no question he could shoot and score. When he got to Chapel Hill, though, he had to learn our system and learn to play defense all over again.

Coach Smith did something with Donald that year that some people questioned—he played him at point guard, when Donald's natural position was two-guard. There was a reason for that. Donald learned what it was like to face pressure by having Derrick coming after him every day in practice. He learned how to play defense by having to guard the point guard every day. His ball-handling and defensive skills developed much more at the point than they would have otherwise.

Over the summer, Donald regained some of the confidence he lost. There were times when he'd get hot and make everything. I think everyone knew toward the end of the summer that Donald was going to have a great year.

When classes started, we continued gathering mid-afternoon at the gym to lift weights and play pick-up games. We also had to make that horrible run up Laurel Hill Road. This is a beautiful neighborhood not far from

This photo from the 1982 Final Four in New Orleans was doctored by the Tar Heel coaching staff. It planted a seed in the players' minds that grew all season long.

the Smith Center, but it's up, up, up, up. Every time you turn a corner you see another hill. That's one good thing about graduating—Laurel Hill's out of my life forever.

We got to know the freshmen better, and they all seemed to fit in well. You get a first impression of someone on a recruiting visit, and you hope that turns out correctly. You hope no one will come in with a bad attitude and cause problems. None of these guys did.

Larry Davis showed from day one how great an athlete and scorer he is, and he began working hard to refine that talent to what it

needs to be for Carolina. Dante Calabria has a chance to be a Jeff Lebo kind of player; he's got a sweet shot. Ed Geth is an easy-going guy who everyone took to immediately. He's a relentless rebounder and has a great future. And Serge Zwikker, once the decision was made to red-shirt him, showed a great attitude to begin spending long hours in the weight room.

An interesting thing happened in early fall. Of course, the coaches can't watch us at all before Nov. 1, but Coach Smith apparently got word that there was a lot of sloppy basketball being played during those full-court games,

NA SUPERDOME

drop by, like J.R. Reid or Kenny Smith. Then we could go fullcourt. Otherwise, it was halfcourt only. Coach's reasoning was pretty simple, actually. You have to work harder in a halfcourt game. In fullcourt, you can out-run your guy to the basket for a layup. On defense, you can hang back a trip. You can get more "street ball" in a fullcourt game, which isn't what Carolina basketball is about. In halfcourt, your man on defense is already there, so you have to work harder to get open. There are no fast-breaks, so you have to play defense every single basket.

Finally, the beginning of practice rolled around. Someone suggested having our first practice at midnight on Nov. 1, and Coach said okay. It was a lot of fun. It was a pretty interesting atmosphere, with people coming to the gym in Halloween costumes. There were goblins and vampires and monsters all over the place. Each of the seniors spoke to the crowd, and Henrik's talk stood out the most.

Henrik got up and said, "If this team plays up to its capabilities, it could be *scarrrrry.*" The combination of all the masks and costumes and Henrik's accent cracked us all up.

It was obvious when practice started we were going to have a lot of intense competition. One drill that became the most concentrated was our four-on-four defense drill, and I think it set the tone for the kind of defense we would play all year. We'd have three teams of four players each, and after a round-robin, the team with the fewest baskets allowed got to watch while the other guys ran sprints. Those battles were fierce. They were taken very, very seriously. The second half of our Florida State game at home, when we came from 22 points down to win, was like that every day. Sometimes at halftime of a game, Coach might say, "If you'd play as hard as you do in practice, we'd be 15 ahead."

At the beginning of practice on Nov. 1, the coaches handed out photos of the basketball court at the New Orleans Superdome with the words, "1993 NCAA Champions North Carolina." Everyone put one in his locker, and I think most everyone took one home. I put one on our refrigerator at the apartment. Several times a day, every day, we were reminded of what our ultimate goal for the year was. Nothing else would do.

"Are we there yet?" became something of a rallying cry for this team and sometimes was Coach Smith's thought for the day, which we had to memorize, along with offensive and defensive points-of-emphasis, before each practice.

Are we there yet?

We knew the answer would be "No" until we cut down the nets in New Orleans. ■

and he instituted a new rule: Four-on-four halfcourt games only.

This upset a lot of guys at first. Some quit coming for about a week. Coach was concerned there was too much dunking, too many behind-the-back passes, too much *junk.* In one of our senior meetings, we brought it up with Coach. One of our concerns was, "Coach, we're not getting in shape playing halfcourt."

He was pretty quick with a response: "Don't worry. *I'll* get you shape come November first."

So we kept playing four-on-four halfcourt, except when some of the pro players would

Wenstrom had eight points and fire in his eyes during scoring flurry in first half of Florida State game in January.

Personalities Loosen Heels On, Off Court.

BY MATT WENSTROM

The 1992-93 Tar Heels will always be remembered as a collection of great basketball players. What many people couldn't see, however, was that this was a team of fascinating characters. The personalities meshed off the court as well as the talents did on the court. There's no doubt that was a major influence on our team developing the chemistry all championship teams have.

We were a very loose team. We were focused and

Please turn to Page 24

One of the last human freedoms is to choose one's attitude in any given circumstance.

serious when the opening tap went up each game but were always relaxed and having fun until then. I think Carolina basketball is an outstanding mixture of discipline and free-wheeling fun. We may look to the public like we're the "IBM of college basketball," as some people call us. We're also the "Toys 'R Us." It's like Coach Smith says, "The disciplined person in society is the free person." We're given a very disciplined structure in which to function that, in turn, provides us the freedom to be ourselves.

Basketball might be our favorite sport, but a close second would certainly be the great game

Wenstrom Exploring Hoops Opportunities.

There are plenty of professional basketball opportunities for 7-footers who are strong, agile and hard-workers. Matt Wenstrom hopes to latch onto one of those chances, either in the NBA or abroad.

"All I can guarantee any team is that I'll be at work every day," says Wenstrom. "I don't have great stats from college because of who was playing ahead of me. But I'll work hard and if given a chance, I think I can prove I deserve a spot on a team somewhere."

Wenstrom was a standout prep player at Mayde Creek High in Houston, Texas, and chose the Tar Heels after an intense recruiting process with a number of top schools. Though he played in the shadow of Scott Williams and Eric Montross during his Tar Heel career, Wenstrom was instrumental in developing the Carolina inside game with his spirited, aggressive play in practice.

He shot 57 percent from the field as a senior and 53 percent for his career, and his career scoring high was 21 points against Cornell in December, 1991. Wenstrom graduated in May with a degree in political science.

of "cracking." There's nothing quite so sweet as a well-chosen wisecrack that hits its mark.

This was an enterprise avidly pursued by everyone on our team, 24 hours a day. There were no holds barred. There was nothing off-limits. If you had a girlfriend, she got cracked on. Body parts got cracked on. Anything was fair game. Usually we kept it above the belt, although there was an occasional low blow.

I take pride in knowing not only were we the best team in the country, but probably the goofiest as well.

Pat Sullivan was one of the team's MVPs in the area of cracking. One of his favorite targets was Henrik Rödl. Sometimes Pat would look at Henrik and reel off every German word he'd ever heard, something that made no sense at all, like "Fahrvergnugen Wiener schnitzel auf Wiedersehen." Henrik would just shake his head and wonder if Pat belonged in a padded room. Pat's trying to pick up some Dutch words now so he carry on the tradition with Serge Zwikker next year.

Henrik hated it when some announcer

would butcher his name. The guy might say, "HINE-rik Ro-DELL," which would steam Henrik no end. For the next day, of course, every time Pat would see Henrik he'd say, "Hello, HINE-rik Ro-DELL."

We gave Dante Calabria a lot of grief early in the year about his sideburns, which came down nearly to his ear lobe, and we stayed on him pretty much all the time about his primping. He's got to be just perfect before he goes out for a game. One day he wore this white suit with a teal shirt, and we started calling him "Pimp Daddy." We really got on poor Dante over that. I felt kind of bad because we didn't see the white suit again—until New Orleans. Then he had a purple shirt with it. He said all along the suit wasn't white, but it sure looked white to us.

Nicknames were a great source of entertainment. Donald Williams was called "Sports Illustrated" early in the year, because he'd just deliver once a week. At the end of the year, though, he was "The New York Times," because his great offensive game would show up every day. A lineup of Scott Cherry, Kevin Salvadori, Henrik, Pat, and myself was "The Cracker Crew," for obvious reasons.

Eric Montross and Travis Stephenson are avid fishermen, so Scott took to calling them Babe Winkleman and Orlando Wilson, after two guys he'd seen do fishing shows on cable TV. Scott cannot for the life of him figure out why anyone would want to spend hour after hour on a boat waiting for a fish to bite. Travis also has a big head—literally—so we call him the Dome Ranger, after the Syracuse Carrier Dome mascot that has a head bigger than a pumpkin. Seriously, those caps that are "one-size-fit-all" barely fit Travis.

Music is another big source of abuse. Eric, Travis and I are country music fans, and most everybody else likes rap. The rap guys crack on us that in country someone's gotten drunk and wrecked the car or beat up on his wife or had an affair with three sisters or something. Then one of us will shoot right back that that's not as bad as all the drugs and violence in rap music.

Movies and TV commercials are good fodder for jokes. We watched some movies on the road over and over and got to where we'd memorize lines out of them. We had a lot of lines out of *The Breakfast Club* and *Wayne's World*. Another favorite was *Hoosiers*, the 1986 film based on the true story of tiny Hickory High winning the 1951 Indiana state championship and beating a lot of big schools in the process. When we went to Indianapolis to play Butler for Eric's homecoming game, the game was played in the same arena where the state championship is held every year and where the state final in *Hoosiers* was filmed. Eric's grandfather was a radio announcer in the real game that *Hoosiers* was based on. Before that game we were reciting lines from the movie, particularly from the scene where they run the "swinging gate" play to get a man open for the winning shot.

It's funny the things that will cross an athlete's mind at the weirdest moments. There's one part in *Hoosiers* where the little kid, Ollie, who's ridden the bench all year, gets chased and fouled in the last seconds of the regional final. He has to make two foul shots to win the game, which he does by heaving them underhanded. When Pat got fouled at the end of the Michigan game, he said he had a fleeting thought walking to the foul line that he was Ollie, having to win the game in *Hoosiers*.

We're also big on picking out lines from TV commercials. We love that one where the kid's playing basketball on the playground, misses the shot and looks around. Then he jumps up and shouts, "He was fouled!" Sometimes in practice, if someone throws up a brick or an airball, he'll look around, flail his arms and yell, "He was fouled!"

We had a lot of fun with little pet superstitions that most everyone on the team has. I insisted, for example, on sitting on the fourth seat on the left on every bus we rode. I put two sticks of yellow gum in my left sock every game (that's Juicy Fruit, but we called all gums by their colors, not their names) and my mouthpiece in my right sock. I wore the same, beat-up old pair of shoes all year. Scott played the same music before each game, beginning with Jam by Michael Jackson and continuing with luminaries from American music such as Hip Hop Hurray by Naughty by Nature. Travis even crossed the line before games and listened to Scott's rap music. Scott also was the last one to pick up his uniform from our equipment manager before home games—no matter how late it was. And Derrick Phelps was the last one to get dressed. Sometimes he'd be listening to music and we'd say, "Derrick, are you going to dress tonight?"

One of the funniest superstitions that arose during the march to the NCAA title was that Travis's mother, Helen, found a heads-up penny entering Joel Coliseum in Winston-Salem before the ECU game. After we won the game, she insisted every game after that on finding a heads-up penny in the arena. She found one minutes before we tipped off against Michigan in Superdome; what she didn't realize was Travis's father, Gene, had been

HUGH MORTON

When not soaring for dunks, Pat Sullivan was deft with a barb.

The Preliminaries:
Good News, Bad News

The regular season and ACC Tournament laid the foundation to the Tar Heels' post-season drive to the NCAA championship. Carolina posted a 26-3 mark and collected the ACC regular-season title with a 14-2 record. The ACC Tournament title fell just beyond the Tar Heels' reach, however, as Georgia Tech notched a 77-75 stunner. A few scenes of the season (clockwise from left): George Lynch dunking, Eric Montross exulting, freshmen Larry Davis, Ed Geth and Dante Calabria learning, Dean Smith and Lenny Wirtz chatting and Derrick Phelps defending.

BOB DONNAN (6)

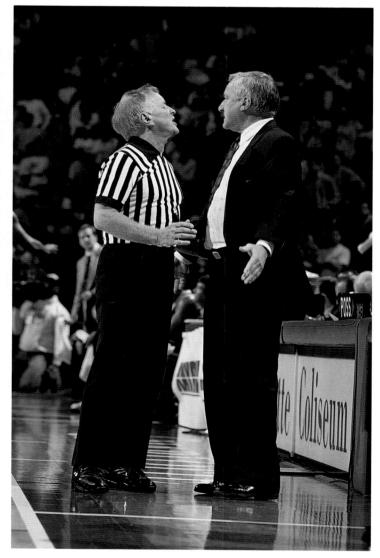

discreetly tossing pennies ahead of them, hoping his wife would find one and that it would be heads-up.

All of our clowning and cracking was done in good fun and within the overall context of what we're at Carolina for: get a degree, number one, and win basketball games, number two. We get away with it because we all like each other and get along so well. You can't joke around with people unless there's a real affection among all of them. We know each other so well, there's not much you can get away without hearing about it. You just have to suck it up, take the abuse and come up with something better yourself.

I knew coming into the season we'd be a better team than we were a year ago. We lost Hubert Davis, who was a great, great scorer. But I knew how well Donald Williams was shooting. You knew scoring would not be a problem. I knew we were good. All we needed was a little edge, a little luck. That's eventually what happened. Every championship team gets breaks. You just have to be there when the breaks come. People talk about the "luck" we got with Chris Webber calling the timeout Michigan didn't have in the NCAA championship game. Maybe we *made* our luck by forcing them with good defense to waste a

timeout earlier in the second half. Maybe we *made* our luck with a great double-team by Derrick and George Lynch that forced a super athlete to panic.

Obviously, your goal every year if you've been a reserve is to get more playing time, and that certainly was mine coming into the season. I'm not a gym rat and have never claimed to be, but I spent more time in the off-season than I have in the past playing ball, running and lifting weights. Beyond that, my goal was to help the team in whatever manner I could. In the final analysis, that's where I contributed the most—giving Eric a war every day in practice that would help him in games.

One of Coach Smith's thoughts for the day was, "One of the last human freedoms is to choose one's attitude in any given circumstance." Each of us had the power to choose, every day, what kind of attitude we would take onto the court. We could have a bad attitude if we lost the night before or if someone had a bad game or if someone wasn't getting the minutes he wanted. We could also make the best of any situation, which this team did very well, all season long. Coach is very big into the mental side of the game. He feels you can push the human body only so far physically and that the next great frontier in coaching will be the

Bloodied Phelps Holds Tar Heels, Self Together.

He soaked in whirlpools, sat with heating pads. He took aspirin and struggled to sleep. There was a brace on his knee, a pad on his elbow and for a while a fluffy pad on his left backside. There was even a blister on his right foot.

Through it all, Derrick Phelps kept playing.

"You just have to keep playing, no matter how you feel," Phelps said the week of the Final Four. "It could be our last game. I just try to play."

The injury woes of Phelps, the Tar Heels' gifted junior point guard, kept Tar Heel fans popping the Tums all winter. There were the two slams on break-away layups, one at Florida State that injured the elbow and another against Virginia in the ACC Tournament that banged up the tailbone and forced Phelps to the bench for the finale. There was a strained knee and an injured hip as well.

Phelps fought through the pain, nonetheless, and had a sterling year passing, directing the Carolina offense and shutting down opposition scoring dynamos. He led the team in assists with 196, was second to George Lynch in steals and was third in rebounds (he had 15 games with five or more rebounds).

Despite playing the East Regional under duress, Phelps committed only four turnovers in two games and silenced Cincinnati's Nick Van Exel in the second half of a 75-68 overtime win.

"Derrick is our best defender," said Brian Reese. "You can tell when he's on someone. It is really hard for that guy to get going.

"Derrick can dominate a game and score only two points," Reese said.

"It has been a rough stretch," Phelps acknowledged. "It's not that I go out there looking to get injured. It just happens. I don't know why. But it's something I have to deal with, and I'm dealing with it pretty well."

Reese, his roommate, noted Phelps' importance to the team and helped push him through the difficult times—in no uncertain terms.

"I tell him straight up, 'If something's broke, fine, you can't play. I understand. But anything short of a broken bone, hey, you're getting out there. You're playing,'" Reese said. "Pain doesn't matter. Not now. Not at this time of the year. The game's too important. Derrick's too important."

When Phelps reinjured his hip in the Kansas game in the Final Four semifinals and came to the bench for several minutes, Dean Smith asked Reese for his thoughts.

"'You know him better than anyone else, Brian. Can he play?'" Reese recalled. "I told Coach, 'Yeah, he's ready. Put him back in. Put him back in *now*.'"

Reese grinned.

"Coach asked me, and *then* he asked Derrick," he said.

mental side of the game.

We were really competitive among ourselves in practice. Eric, Kevin and I killed each other every day. There were a lot of collisions in the paint, a lot of pushing and hitting. It had to have helped Eric in a game, because what he got in practice from Kevin and me was as rough as what he saw from anyone else.

Basketball players never get as much playing time as they'd like. Most people would like to play 40 minutes. Sure, I would have liked to play more than I did. But Eric was getting the job done for us, and Kevin was doing a great job off the bench with what he does best—defense and blocking shots. Kevin's arms are longer than mine and Eric's, and he's a quicker jumper. That's what makes him so intimidating as a shot-blocker. And we were winning. It's hard to make noise about playing time if you're only losing four games a year. I could have gone somewhere else and had more points and rebounds after four years, but I wouldn't have gotten as well-rounded an experience as I did at Carolina. I pledged Pi Kappa Alpha fraternity as a sophomore and enjoyed that experience very much. I'm a firm believer there's more to life than basketball.

The season started well, beginning with a 119-82 win over Old Dominion. Then we swept the field at the Diet Pepsi Tournament of Champions in Charlotte, deciding even then to pass up the traditional net cutting to wait for April. We had good road wins at Roanoke against Virginia Tech, at Butler and at Ohio State before we broke to go home for Christmas.

The holiday trip to Hawaii for the Rainbow Classic was good for helping build the *esprit de corps* that we enjoyed all year. It also gave the freshmen a chance to see how the team operated together, and I think they probably came out of the trip with a higher comfort level of being part of the team.

We each traveled separately to Honolulu after spending a couple of days with our families, and as much as we enjoyed seeing our

HUGH MORTON

real families at Christmas, it was fun convening in Hawaii with all the guys. Being in the company of each other made us feel like we really were home.

It rained a lot that week, so we had to spend most of our time in our rooms. We'd get 10 or 12 guys in one room, playing nickel poker, watching movies, cracking on each other. When the weather did break, we got out and rode mopeds or went swimming.

One day a bunch of us were out swimming,

Virginia came to Chapel Hill Jan. 20 unbeaten, riding a 16-game win streak and happy with an upset of Duke three days before. But the Tar Heels, with Kevin Salvadori's 14 points leading the scoring, claimed an easy 80-59 win.

Days Of Wine And Cheeses

Two wins over Florida State added spice to the season: Carolina's just taken the lead (below) as Donald Williams runs the delay after 22-point rally in Chapel Hill. Seconds later, the Smith Center crowd went nuts. A month later in Tallahassee, Brian Reese's scoring and rebounding landed him on the cover of "Sports Illustrated."

Smooth Head, Sweet Stroke Give Williams Lethal Look.

Short hair works for Eric Montross. So Donald Williams thought he'd go one better—no hair.

Williams had his head shaved the Thursday before the Final Four. What long hair did for Sampson, no hair worked wonders for Williams. He hit 15-of-23 field goals and 10-of-14 three-pointers in two games and was named MVP of the Final Four.

"I'm going to get my hair cut like this all the time," Williams said after the 77-71 championship win over Michigan.

Williams made three 3-pointers and another baseline jumper in the last 10 minutes of the championship game and followed those up with four foul shots in the last 11 seconds. Two of those clinched the win after a technical foul on Michigan.

"I didn't want to put any pressure on myself," Williams said. "My teammates were very confident. I thought, 'I'll just shoot these like I'm in a gym by myself.'"

Williams' last 3-pointer came with 4:12 left and Michigan up by four. The Tar Heels passed the ball inside, Michigan sloughed off around Montross, who kicked the ball back outside to Derrick Phelps on the left, who whipped it across to Williams on the right.

"We were trying to move the ball and kill some time by making them work without the ball," Williams said. "Derrick found me on a cross-court pass, and I knocked it down."

It was quite a show, which Dean Smith made appropriate note of.

"He was in a different zone out there." Smith said. "I thought he was going to make it every time he put it up. And I think the other team did, too."

Williams rebounded from a difficult freshman season in which he averaged 2.2 points in playing the No. 2 point-guard slot behind Phelps. This year, he went back to the two-guard spot, and, with a year's experience, blossomed in every respect. His average soared to 13.9 for the season—19.6 during the six games of the NCAA Tournament. After a 4-of-18 performance against Georgia Tech in the ACC Tournament final, he scored nine, 17, 22 and 20 points leading to his Final Four explosions of 25 each night.

"I never could have imagined this," Williams said, flashing a grin in the euphoria of the Tar Heel lockerroom. "I mean, every little kid dreams about making game-winning shots and stuff, but truthfully, last year all this didn't seem possible."

and several other guys had rented two pontoon boats. I think it was George, Brian, Pat, Derrick and Donald. They started riding toward us and realized they made a mistake. We charged them, caught them and sunk the pontoon boat—with these guys in their street clothes with their wallets and watches. Everyone got a good laugh out of that.

We lost to Michigan by one point in the semifinals when Jalen Rose picked up a rebound with one second to go and threw it in. That game showed us we could compete with anyone. It's one thing to feel confident. It's another to prove it. To lose by one point, to

Michigan, on a fluke shot at the buzzer, that's nothing to be upset about. It showed everyone we were for real.

We played pretty good basketball when we came home up until the first half of the Florida State game at the Smith Center. The bad news was we were down by 45-28 at halftime. The good news was I'd gotten to play six minutes and scored eight points and had three offensive rebounds. Eric, who had three fouls early, came back in the second half and played most of the way, but it was nice to have contributed to a stretch in the first half when we settled down somewhat and got our feet under us.

The second-half comeback was one of the season's highlights. You can never give up at halftime no matter what the score because, if one team has a great half and can outscore the other by 17, the same thing can reverse itself in the second.

We were down by 20 with 9:36 to play when Henrik hit two 3-pointers and Donald made two jumpers. That ignited our rally. The run was capped by George stealing a pass near halfcourt on a trap and slamming it home to give us the lead with 1:41 to play. George is so quick, he could just about free-lance out there. Sometimes he'd guard every player on the floor because he was running around so much, trapping everyone. George was drooling, sitting back waiting for that pass. That was typical George Lynch. We held them off for an 82-77 win. The crowd mobbed the floor after the game, and we celebrated like we'd won the ACC Tournament or something.

Then we lost two in a row—an 88-62 blowout at Wake Forest and an 81-67 loss at Duke. It seemed like a lot of us just weren't ready to play the Wake Forest game. The Florida State game had taken a lot out of us, and I think we were in kind of a midseason lull. They really played well and just wore us out. We played pretty well the next Wednesday at Duke, but they pulled away the last four minutes to win the game.

That week did a lot to sober us up and reinforce some things we needed to keep uppermost in our minds. We saw that we were never out of a game, that anything was possible. We were reminded that we've got to be ready to play every night, or a good team like Wake Forest could kill us. And the Duke game was testament to playing all-out for 40 minutes. We only showed up for 36 minutes that night. That was a difficult stretch. You play Florida State, Wake and Duke three games in a row, you're going to get some blemishes.

The second time around with those three teams showed how much we had progressed and developed in just one month. The 86-76 win in Tallahassee was huge. That gave us a lot of momentum. That win clinched at least a tie for first in the regular-season standings. That was the most intense game of the year. It was their Senior Day, and they started Bob Sura, a sophomore, ahead of one of their seniors. That showed how much they wanted to win.

It was an incredibly physical game, people diving for loose balls, throwing elbows, talking to each other. There were even a couple of technical fouls. Brian Reese had probably the best game of his career, scoring 25 points and six in a row during a 10-0 run in the second half that broke open a tie game. He had two drives against Florida State's 2-3 zone that I wish could somehow be framed and matted for posterity.

That was one of our sweeter wins. In the lockerroom after the game, you could see how much it meant to everyone. We were singing the Seminole war chant and doing the tomahawk chop. Like Eric said, "We're not exactly best friends." Derrick had a frightening fall when he got hammered by Rodney Dobard on a layup, but fortunately he only suffered a bruised elbow and was back for the Wake Forest game. We really wanted to play well down there. It showed we were ready. It was like a tournament game—on the road, against a quality team.

After the game in Tallahassee, we came home to wrap the schedule up with Wake Forest and Duke. We won both rather handily, beating Wake by 18 and Duke by 14. Winning on Senior Day over Duke was another highlight, especially since my parents were up from Texas for the game.

This was a unique season in that all the teams that had beaten us in big games recently, we had a chance to return the favor. I call this "The Payback Season."

Three years ago, Arkansas beat us in the NCAAs. We beat them this year.

Our sophomore year, Kansas beat us in the Final Four. We beat them, too.

Last year, Ohio State knocked us out of the NCAAs. We beat them as well.

Also last year, Florida State beat us twice in the regular season and Sam Cassell had his little "wine-and-cheese" remark. We beat them in the ACC Tournament last year and then twice this season. I think we've settled that score.

Then this year, Wake Forest and Duke beat us earlier in the year, and we won the next time.

And then there's that little matter of avenging a loss to Michigan back in December in the Rainbow Classic . . . ∎

HUGH MORTON

Nice way to end the year: Eric Montross thunders dunk home against Duke in 83-69 Senior Day win.

Cherry (second from left above), mates hold hands, then explode during crucial foul shots in East Regional.

Winston Romp, Jersey War Clinch Final Four.

BY SCOTT CHERRY

It was almost 7 p.m. when we boarded the bus outside the Charlotte Coliseum after losing to Georgia Tech in the final of the ACC Tournament. Everyone was down about the game. We felt we had the better team—we'd won two earlier games by a 24-point total—but without Derrick Phelps playing, we just weren't quite in synch. Winning the tournament had been one of our goals for the season, and now it was gone.

The loss was particularly disappointing personally

Please turn to Page 36

We're on the right track. But if we stand still, we could get run over.

because, with Derrick out, it was up to the other point guards to overcome his absence. We all played hard and did some good things, but obviously not enough to win. Plus, Georgia Tech played a tremendous game. James Forrest was like a house afire and we couldn't cool him off. They won, 77-75.

That loss hammered home the fact that injuries are a part of the game, that maybe Derrick might not get back at all. That meant everybody would have to pick up his intensity, renew his dedication toward our ultimate goal of winning the NCAA championship. We had to rebound harder, play defense tougher, work

off and be ready to go back to work Tuesday. "This is still a special team," he said. "Great things will still happen if we pull together and work hard."

No matter how many games we'd won so far, none meant anything if we didn't win the last six. One thought for the day that popped up occasionally went like this: "We're on the right track. But if we stand still, we could get run over." So what if we beat Florida State twice and Duke at home to end the regular season? So what if we won the ACC regular season? If we didn't keep improving, those teams and 10 others across the country would catch up and pass us by.

Coach Smith stresses that we're not playing in a 64-team NCAA field—rather, we're playing in a four-team weekend tournament that we *have* to win. If we win this one, we can play another one. As we gathered for practice on Tuesday, there were only four teams left in the world as far as we were concerned: Carolina, East Carolina, Rhode Island and Purdue. Our job was to go to Winston-Salem and prevail over those three teams.

With two good performances, we expected to win both of our games that weekend, but we never dreamed we'd have as easy a time as we did, beating East Carolina 85-65 and Rhode Island 112-67. Both teams looked good on tape, and both had to have some good wins to get where they were. East Carolina was difficult to shake. You could see how fired up they were, getting a chance to play us, and they were hot from outside in the first half. But we had too much height and firepower and got a good win to open the tournament.

The Rhode Island game was one of the strangest I've ever been around. I thought it would be a tough game. But we dominated so much early they were totally taken out of it mentally. You could see it in the eyes of their point guard. Every time he came downcourt he was waiting to get trapped. No one wanted the ball. They missed some open shots near the basket because they were so worried about our height advantage. Some of our guys said at halftime they were saying things on the foul line like, "You guys are good" or "Take it easy, man."

We loved the big lead on the bench because the starters came out early in the second half and the rest of us got some quality minutes in an NCAA Tournament game. That was a lot of

Triangle Influence Heavy In NCAA Championship.

The NCAA basketball title has resided in the ACC—not to mention the Triangle—for five of the last 12 years.

The Tar Heels have two titles (1982 and 1993), Duke two (1991 and 1992) and N.C. State has one (1983). During that period, the Big 10 and Big East have each won two titles, with the Big West, Big 8 and Metro winning one each.

Other trivia from the NCAAs:

* Dean Smith is now the fourth active coach to have won two or more titles, the others being Bob Knight of Indiana (1976, 1981 and 1987), Denny Crum of Louisville (1980 and 1986) and Duke's Mike Krzyzewski.

* Smith has the all-time lead in NCAA Tournament wins with 55, and his nine Final Four teams is second to UCLA's John Wooden with 12.

* Carolina has three national titles, with only UCLA (10), Kentucky (five) and Indiana (five) ahead.

* Carolina's 34-win season bolted Smith ahead of Phog Allen, Ed Diddle and Hank Iba on the all-time victory list. His 774 wins trails Adolph Rupp's 875 total.

* The Tar Heels now have a nine-win lead over Kentucky in the all-time school victory column. Carolina has 1,570, Kentucky 1,561.

more to get open on the offensive end. Whether Derrick came back or not, we simply had to be more focused. Winning 28 games and the ACC regular-season title meant nothing now. The bright spot of losing was that Georgia Tech had given us a wake-up call.

As we settled into our seats, some of us turned on radios and little TVs, and we started to pick up on the pairings for the NCAAs. The mood lightened. We ate pizza and began to look ahead. Just as our heads would have come off a high had we won, we started pulling them out of the dumps and directing our thoughts toward winning six more games.

We figured we'd still get the No. 1 East seed and open in Winston-Salem, and the rumor was we'd play East Carolina. That's exactly what happened. We looked around to see where the other ACC teams were going. Virginia, also in the East, would be the only ACC team we could meet before the Final Four. By the time we got back to Chapel Hill, the loss was a thing of the past. Coach Guthridge told us to take Monday

Tar Heels' Road To The Title

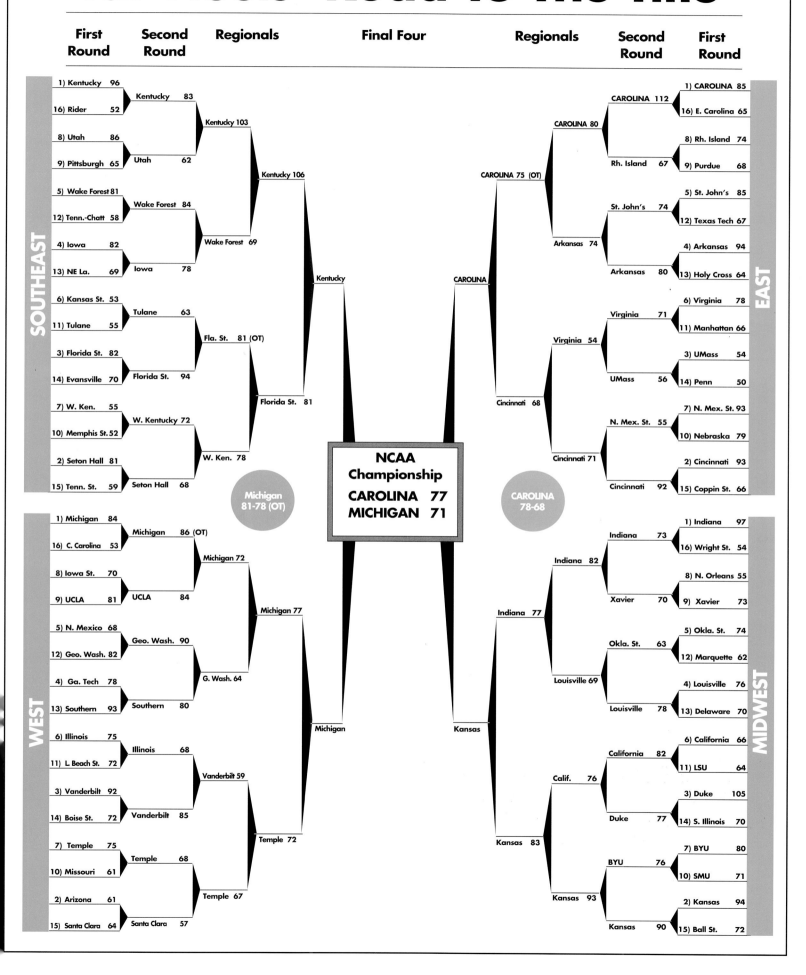

| First Round | Second Round | Regionals | Final Four | Regionals | Second Round | First Round |

SOUTHEAST

1) Kentucky 96
16) Rider 52
— Kentucky 83

8) Utah 86
9) Pittsburgh 65
— Utah 62

Kentucky 103

5) Wake Forest 81
12) Tenn.-Chatt 58
— Wake Forest 84

4) Iowa 82
13) NE La. 69
— Iowa 78

Wake Forest 69

Kentucky 106

6) Kansas St. 53
11) Tulane 55
— Tulane 63

3) Florida St. 82
14) Evansville 70
— Florida St. 94

Fla. St. 81 (OT)

7) W. Ken. 55
10) Memphis St. 52
— W. Kentucky 72

2) Seton Hall 81
15) Tenn. St. 59
— Seton Hall 68

W. Ken. 78

Florida St. 81

Kentucky

Michigan 81-78 (OT)

WEST

1) Michigan 84
16) C. Carolina 53
— Michigan 86 (OT)

8) Iowa St. 70
9) UCLA 81
— UCLA 84

Michigan 72

5) N. Mexico 68
12) Geo. Wash. 82
— Geo. Wash. 90

4) Ga. Tech 78
13) Southern 93
— Southern 80

G. Wash. 64

Michigan 77

6) Illinois 75
11) L. Beach St. 72
— Illinois 68

3) Vanderbilt 92
14) Boise St. 72
— Vanderbilt 85

Vanderbilt 59

7) Temple 75
10) Missouri 61
— Temple 68

2) Arizona 61
15) Santa Clara 64
— Santa Clara 57

Temple 67

Temple 72

Michigan

NCAA Championship
CAROLINA 77
MICHIGAN 71

CAROLINA 78-68

EAST

1) CAROLINA 85
16) E. Carolina 65
— CAROLINA 112

8) Rh. Island 74
9) Purdue 68
— Rh. Island 67

CAROLINA 80

5) St. John's 85
12) Texas Tech 67
— St. John's 74

4) Arkansas 94
13) Holy Cross 64
— Arkansas 80

Arkansas 74

CAROLINA 75 (OT)

6) Virginia 78
11) Manhattan 66
— Virginia 71

3) UMass 54
14) Penn 50
— UMass 56

Virginia 54

7) N. Mex. St. 93
10) Nebraska 79
— N. Mex. St. 55

2) Cincinnati 93
15) Coppin St. 66
— Cincinnati 92

Cincinnati 71

Cincinnati 68

CAROLINA

MIDWEST

1) Indiana 97
16) Wright St. 54
— Indiana 73

8) N. Orleans 55
9) Xavier 73
— Xavier 70

Indiana 82

5) Okla. St. 74
12) Marquette 62
— Okla. St. 63

4) Louisville 76
13) Delaware 70
— Louisville 78

Louisville 69

Indiana 77

6) California 66
11) LSU 64
— California 82

3) Duke 105
14) S. Illinois 70
— Duke 77

Calif. 76

7) BYU 80
10) SMU 71
— BYU 76

2) Kansas 94
15) Ball St. 72
— Kansas 90

Kansas 93

Kansas 83

Kansas

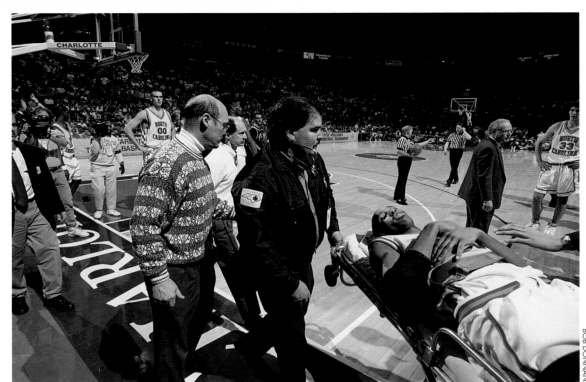

Phelps was carried from the court on a stretcher following his ACC Tournament injury against Virginia. Two weeks later, however, his second-half defense bottled up Cincinnati's Nick Van Exel.

BOB DONNAN

HUGH MORTON

fun. I wasn't about to give the tired signal and risk coming out. You could hear the fans were having a good time cheering for us.

The starters were giving Travis Stephenson a hard time on the bench. Travis and I always sat in the last two seats at the end of the bench, and every time the bench stood up, someone took Travis's seat and pushed him up closer to the coaches. Travis played about five minutes, and the crowd was going crazy for him to shoot. That was about the loudest the crowd got the whole game. Unfortunately, he was a little too far out when he got the ball in the last few seconds and couldn't repeat his buzzer-beater from the Duke game.

There was one moment in the East Carolina game that gave us all a scare. Derrick hadn't practiced that week after suffering a badly bruised tailbone against Virginia in the ACC semifinals. He was wearing a protective pad, and when he first went in the game midway through the first half, he made a quick steal and gave us a big lift. Then in the second half, East Carolina got a breakaway layup, and Derrick was the only man back on defense. We were kind of saying to ourselves on the bench, "Let him go, Derrick, let him go." But that's not Derrick's nature. He stood right in there and took the charge and went sprawling on his backside. We held our breath for a minute, but he got right up. Derrick had sacrificed his body all year and he wasn't about to quit now, no matter that we were 20 points up.

Once it became obvious that Derrick's injuries weren't going to keep him out of a game, it was time to start cracking on him. In practice we were teaching Derrick to do layups with two hands and jump from two feet. That way if he got hit, he'd have both feet underneath to catch himself. It was kind of funny because Henrik Rödl, Dante Calabria and I would beat each other to death in practice while Derrick was getting treatment or watching from the sideline, and then he'd play 35 minutes the next game.

There was one memorable practice the Saturday between the Arkansas and Cincinnati games in the East Regional finals in New Jersey.

Derrick wasn't practicing, and Coach Smith was trying to get Henrik, Dante and I ready to play Cincinnati's trapping, fullcourt press by running each of us through the white team (or first team). Henrik would mess up and then he'd rotate Dante in there. Then Dante would make a mistake and he'd put me in. I'd run a couple of plays and foul up. It seemed like whatever we did, we did it wrong. Coach got upset with himself after that practice for being too concerned about what Cincinnati would do, and not worrying about our team. He told us

Injury Bugaboo Bounced, Reese Explodes As Junior.

It was a long haul for Brian Reese. But the 1992-93 season was the one in which his acrobatic athletic skills merged with good health and two years of collegiate experience to produce a key element of the Tar Heels' championship drive.

Reese's raw ability was evident upon his arrival in Chapel Hill two years ago. The challenge was to buff it so that it fit the Tar Heels' highly structured playbook.

Reese was tied up vs. State with an injury.

"Growing up in New York, it was one-on-one," Reese said. "You can see the moves I make, they come from the playground. Somebody is always wanting to try something new on you.

"Then, becoming an All-America in high school, you have to take shots. It's you, you, you. That is the way they put it on you. You have to be 'The Man' every game.

"But here it's different. Everybody's an All-America. Coming to Carolina was a big change for me, mentally and physically. I'm from New York. I never ran a day in my life. Running track? Get in shape? I didn't know what that was. I rode buses, trains, cabs everywhere. Running? I didn't know what that was."

By midseason, Reese had shaken a strained back muscle and sprained ankle and began to flourish. His 25 points (18 in the second half) led Carolina's 86-76 win at Florida State in late February. He had 13 points and eight rebounds against Arkansas in the East Regional semifinals and finished the season with an 11.4 point average (13.4 over the last 15 games).

"It takes some time before you grasp things, but you eventually realize that this approach to basketball has been winning games for a long time," Reese said.

Reese was the only Tar Heel starter who can recall having seen the Tar Heels' 1982 NCAA title win over Georgetown. In fact, it had quite an effect on him.

"I was more of a baseball fan, but I watched the game because Fred Brown was from my neighborhood. He went to school with my brother," Reese said.

"Then I started noticing how North Carolina played, the way they played together. I'd never seen anything like that. Then I got into basketball, and North Carolina was my team from then on. I started wearing North Carolina things, wearing their colors."

that in the meeting later.

So the next day, Derrick came out and played 43 minutes (including an overtime). Dante played one. I cheered from the bench. Derrick heard about that one later.

The East Regional finals in the Meadowlands in New Jersey was another four-team tournament, with us, Arkansas, Cincinnati and Virginia. No matter what we thought going to Winston-Salem a week earlier, we *knew* this weekend would be a challenge. Arkansas and

Cincinnati were both cat-quick, athletic teams like Florida State, the teams that tend to give us trouble. And should we meet Virginia again, we knew we'd beaten them three times this season and a fourth win would be difficult.

We checked into the Park Lane Hotel overlooking Central Park in Manhattan on Thursday. One of the great things about playing basketball for Carolina is that you travel first-class in every respect. The coaches figure that, as hard as we work and as much as we bring to the University in terms of recognition and revenue, without being paid anything beyond our scholarships, we at least ought to stay in the finest hotels and eat the best food. The Park Lane is one of the classiest hotels in the city, and it's a super experience, particularly for guys who haven't been in New York much. We had a team meeting in a big room on the 41st floor, overlooking Central Park, and while all the New York guys were sitting around the table before the meeting began, everyone else was looking out the window, marveling over the view.

The Saturday night between games, the team went to Smith & Wollensky, a famous steakhouse on East 49th Street. Some of the bigger eaters on the team got 32-ounce steaks, which still aren't as big as the 48-ounce steaks Matt Wenstrom and Kevin Salvadori order whenever we go to Morton's, a steakhouse in Georgetown we've been to before Maryland games. Matt complained for two days that he was getting old and couldn't eat that much beef anymore.

The games that weekend were testaments to the adaptability of our team to play uptempo styles, to the individual abilities of each of our starters and key reserves, to our ability to play great defense in key situations and, finally, to the coaching of Dean Smith.

The seniors really wanted to beat Arkansas because they'd beaten us our freshman year in the Final Eight. Scott Williams, a senior that year, called during the week to wish us well. We knew they'd play a fast, uptempo game and would be difficult to beat.

We were mind-boggled by some of the comments coming out of Arkansas during the week. One of their guys said they'd pressure us like we'd never seen before, in our face, 94 feet, for 40 minutes. If they could pressure better than Florida State, we said, bring them on. Their comments were repeated many times during the week. That just fueled the fire already in us.

Our starters would never make statements like that. Sometimes our players are accused of not being real open with the media. That's not true. Our guys try to be as honest as possible. But none of our starters are going to say something stupid that can incite the other team. One of the Cincinnati players said before the regional final that he questioned Coach Smith's ability, having won just one NCAA title with all the talent he'd had. We couldn't believe that. How does a 20-year-old who's hardly accomplished anything knock a Hall of Fame coach who's won more than 700 games? Matt read that quote out of *The New York Times* I'll bet 50 times before that game.

The Arkansas game was just as we figured— nip and tuck, fast-paced, anyone's game. We rallied from 11 down in the first half to tie it at 45 at halftime. There was a flurry of transitions early in the second half that showcased what a wonderful blend of diversified abilities our team had become. Eric Montross made a great pass three-quarters of the court into the corner to Brian Reese, who flew by his man on that lightning-quick first step for a layup. Then Derrick threw another three-quarters court pass ahead to George Lynch for a layup, the ball just missing the outreached hands of an Arkansas guy. George can run the court better than any four-man in the country. Then Eric got the ball on the low block on the left side, and instead of his usual right-handed hook off a move to the left, countered to the right with a turnaround jumper. The only part of this run that didn't fit was an airball by Donald Williams. I don't think we saw any more of those.

Our first big defensive play came with 2:34 left in the game, the Tar Heels up by two. We played tight for 45 seconds and forced them into a hurried, leaning shot with a hand in the

NCAA Title Run Gives Cherry Thrills.

Scott Cherry is a native of upstate New York and drew the attention of the UNC staff when a local TV sportscaster sent a game tape to Chapel Hill during Cherry's senior year. That led to a scouting trip by Bill Guthridge and then a visit from Dean Smith.

The scholarship offer from Smith came as quite a surprise, but it certainly wasn't anything Cherry, a point guard who averaged 20 points a game as a senior at Central Catholic in Saratoga Springs, was going to turn down.

Cherry saw spot duty on the floor throughout his career at Carolina but contributed immeasurably as a friend, leader and inspirational practice player.

Watching tape of the Tar Heels' epic win over Michigan in the NCAA final, Cherry said simply:

"It makes your hair stand on end. To have been a part of something this special is something I'll never forget."

Cherry graduated in May with a degree in business administration and was hoping for an opportunity to continue his playing career in Europe. He's also considering avenues to get into sports administration on either the pro or collegiate levels.

face from about 15 feet as the 45-second clock went off. That was huge. We went down and scored and were up by four.

When Arkansas hit a three-pointer to cut it to 75-74 with 51 seconds left, we called a timeout and listened to Coach Smith go to work.

I don't know how many times we've seen it over the years, and I only have a four-year frame of reference. But Coach set up a play that everyone knew would work and, of course, it worked to perfection. My freshman year, we were playing in Hawaii and he diagramed a play to get King Rice a shot at the buzzer that beat James Madison. The next year, he diagramed one to get Rick Fox a shot to beat Oklahoma to keep our Sweet 16 streak alive. Earlier this year, we held off a late Seton Hall rally on a great "home-run pass" from George to Derrick that Coach designed in the huddle. And later in the tournament, he would use Donald as a decoy, Eric as a screen and set Brian up for an open shot to beat Cincinnati. Unfortunately, the ball slipped out of his hand and Brian missed the dunk, but we won the game anyway in overtime.

Tonight it was a backdoor play from George to Donald. Coach told our guys what to do and what the Arkansas players would do in response. It worked exactly like he drew it up.

George got the ball out above the key, and here a lot of acting came into play. Brian was on the wing, in front of our bench, Donald on the opposite wing. Eric was beside the lane, nearest our bench. The key for this play is for George to act like he's caught and in a hurry to pass it. Both Brian and Eric moved out as if to receive a pass. Eric brought Arkansas center Corliss Williamson with him. The Arkansas players now thought George was in a panic to pass it. George looked over to the other side, and the Arkansas player guarding Donald expected a pass his way and broke in front of Donald to pick it off. So Donald went back door and was wide open, with no one in the lane to pick him up. That's where Eric's move out to supposedly help George was significant. He took his man with him, leaving the lane open for Donald.

Then George made a great defensive play to seal the win, picking up Robert Shepherd on a pick and forcing him into an up-and-down violation. A pick, of course, is designed to free up a man by screening the man guarding him, but George did a textbook job recognizing it and jumping out on Shepherd.

I don't remember exactly when it started, but sometime late in this game the guys on the bench began holding hands during clutch foul-shot situations. When it worked once, we kept it up throughout the rest of the tournament. It was funny watching the tape of last minutes of the Michigan game, when Henrik was trying to get Brian to hold his hand when Pat Sullivan was on the line. Brian wasn't into holding hands too much, plus he was preoccupied with trying to suck blood from a cut on his hand so that the officials wouldn't see it and he could go back in the game.

The Cincinnati game had us a little worried in the first half, when they broke on top by 15 points, 29-14. Nick Van Exel was hitting everything he looked at, including one 3-pointer falling out-of-bounds. We had a hand in his face most of the time, but he still made 6-of-10 three-pointers anyway. Another great move by Coach and another great defensive game by Derrick helped turn things around. Coach told

Derrick at halftime to stay on Van Exel and forget about helping or trapping. Derrick was walking around the lockerroom at half, saying, "He's mine now. He's mine now." That shut Van Exel down and he only got two more points the rest of the game.

A lot was made of Brian missing the dunk at the end of the game, but one of the officials said it wouldn't have counted anyway. It was just one those strange twists the game takes. We were a little stunned when it happened, but George got in everyone's face coming back to the bench, told them we'd still win the game and we were just five minutes from New Orleans. True to his word, George refused to let us lose, and Donald came through with two 3-pointers. When we finally won, 75-68, George was named the MVP with 21 points, 14 rebounds and six steals in the game.

There was a little difference of opinion immediately after the game about whether or not to cut down the nets. A couple of guys wanted to, but several others said no.

"Let's wait until next week," someone said. "We've got more work to do."

We were pleased to have won. But satisfied? No way. ∎

Tar Heels whoop and holler with sportscaster Andrea Joyce following East Regional title.

H. C. 72   MICH. 69   TM.

Rödl reaches to harass Jalen Rose jumper late in NCAA title game; his defense and leadership were keys to Heels' success.

Bourbon St. Agenda: Play First, Party Later.

BY HENRIK RÖDL

New Orleans would be different from Indianapolis. I could feel that Sunday on the trip back from the Meadowlands after winning the NCAA East Regional. And I knew it even more on Tuesday as we gathered for practice after taking Monday off.

We all went crazy two years ago when we beat Temple to earn that trip to the Final Four. It had been nine years since Carolina had been to the Final Four, and the pressure to return had gotten pretty intense. It

Please turn to Page 44

Grant me the serenity to accept the things I cannot change, the courage to change those I can, and the wisdom to know the difference.

seemed like getting to Indianapolis was the victory that year. We practiced hard that week, but it's almost like that whole week was one big victory lap—we were taking a bow for just getting back to the Final Four.

We had three seniors on that team but played a lot of sophomores and freshmen, and we were a little awed by the whole thing. There were more people at the Hoosier Dome to watch practice on Friday than can get into many ACC games—there must have been over 20,000. We didn't handle the whole thing very well and the result, as everyone knows, was a loss to Kansas.

Ten of 15 players on this year's roster were seniors and juniors and had been to Indianapolis, and we approached Final Four week with a much more businesslike demeanor. Our practices were just like they'd been all year—enough cracking on each other to have fun and keep things loose, but when Coach Smith blew the whistle to start practice, it was serious business. That continuity told me we weren't in for any surprises when we got to

Olympics, Final Four Make Big Splash In Rödl Memory.

It's been quite a year for Henrik Rödl. First there were the Olympics in Barcelona, where he represented his native Germany. Then it was an NCAA Championship with the Tar Heels.

"It's been an incredible year for the teams I've been involved with," says Rödl. "The Olympics is a unique experience. It's really not comparable to the NCAAs because you're playing for your country. I had some very special moments with both teams."

Rödl, a native of Heusenstamm, Germany, will return to his native land this summer for 16 months of mandatory service to his country. He'll also play pro basketball in the German league.

After that, Rödl's not sure what the future holds. He graduated with a degree in biology, and medical school and career in sports medicine are possibilities. He says he and Susan will make a decision later whether to continue pro ball in Europe or perhaps return to the States.

Rödl played in 140 games as a Tar Heel, matching George Lynch, Pete Chilcutt, Rick Fox and King Rice for the career record for games played. He had 303 career assists, second highest among active Carolina players and 17th in UNC history.

New Orleans.

The scramble for tickets and hotel rooms started that Monday. All the parents and friends were scared to jinx us by making any plans for New Orleans, so when we won the East Regional everyone was busy helping with arrangements for their families. It was a good problem to have. I didn't have that many requests to take care of. It was too far a trip for my parents in Heusenstamm, Germany. Each player was allotted four tickets, and mine went to Susan, my wife; my best friend, Mark McCombs, a lecturer in the math department at Carolina; and a former teammate from Germany who coincidentally was vacationing in Florida with his wife and wanted to follow us to New Orleans. I also bought two tickets for two former Chapel Hill High teammates, John Kirks and Joel Hackney.

Coach Smith downplayed the rematch with Coach Roy Williams of Kansas from the beginning of the week. That had been a much bigger issue two years ago, when the seniors had been freshmen when Coach Williams was still at Carolina. This year, I was really the only player on the team with any connection to Coach Williams. I was introduced to Carolina basketball about nine years ago when Coach Williams taught at a basketball camp in Germany. He had tapes of Carolina games, and that's when I became a Tar Heel fan and a Michael Jordan fan. I had never experienced anyone who could be friendly but tough as well. I respected him from the outset and wanted to learn more about this place called North Carolina.

We noticed the similarities between the Kansas team and our team. Many of the players were similar. Eric Montross was dubbed "Ostertross" after their big center Greg Ostertag, and we started calling Kevin Salvadori "Kevin Pauley" after the lanky Jayhawk, Eric Pauley, who resembled Sal. We knew in this game of mirror images the outcome would not be decided by Xs and Os but by execution—whoever played the best and the hardest would win.

We didn't leave for New Orleans until Friday morning, Coach preferring we stay in Chapel Hill, practice and go to class and not get all caught up in the hoopla in New Orleans. I think that was a smart thing to do—a *very* smart thing to do. That environment—the bars, the music, the food, the crowds—could make it difficult to concentrate on basketball. We landed in New Orleans, went straight to the Superdome and, after practice and the press conference, we checked into the Hotel Inter-Continental. The atmosphere started to sink in as a jazz band in the lobby was playing our fight song when we arrived. Almost immediately, some of us walked two blocks down St. Charles Avenue, across Canal Street and over to Bourbon Street.

We were able in an hour or so then to see what was going on, get a flavor of the city and all the fans in town and then set it aside. We had work to do. This wasn't a party. There was a lot of drinking and parading going on, and I

Derrick Phelps (L) and Brian Reese meet the press in New Orleans prior to facing Kansas in semifinals.

knew it was something I didn't need to be a part of. I saw all I wanted to see in an hour or so. There would be plenty of time later to go to Bourbon Street and have fun. The thing I've learned about these basketball trips is that, whether you're going to Hawaii or Iowa, the fun trips are the ones when you win. Rick Pitino and Steve Fisher brought their teams in on Wednesday. I wonder how much fun they had at the Final Four.

Coach occasionally will put us in a hotel away from the crowd if he's worried about distractions. We stayed well out of town in Indianapolis in '91, but New Orleans was so jammed full with people there wasn't any place else for us to go. So we stayed at the Carolina-designated hotel, with our athletic department staff, Educational Foundation group and fans. Our fans are great, don't get me wrong. But it was a change having to sign autographs every time you went for a team meal or got off an elevator. It was especially difficult for guys like George Lynch and Eric. I give those guys a lot of credit for being patient with all the fans' requests and still being able to keep their focus and not get sidetracked.

We had an optional shooting practice at the Superdome Saturday morning. Game-day practices are very loose and informal. Some of the guys have little games they'll play with each other—like Scott Cherry and I have a 3-point shooting contest each game—but mainly they're just to loosen up and kill some time. How much bearing they have on a game is questionable. Donald missed the shoot-around because room service had yet to deliver his breakfast, but he passed on most all year. They really are "optional," and Donald didn't need the practice, anyway.

A lot of the guys on the team have little superstitions and rituals they go through before games, and Coach Smith comments sometimes on getting letters from people who say they wear the same underwear or sit in the same chairs or whatever during games. Travis Stephenson and Pat Sullivan picked up on Coach Williams' "spit-for-good-luck" in the Mississippi River and deposited a couple of hawks in the river on Saturday.

Personally, I stay away from superstition. I simply believe that God has already

determined the outcome, that it's already on the books. That's one thing that helps me shake my pregame nervousness. I get peace knowing that I can take a great attitude onto the court and play hard, but the outcome is already decided.

That brings to mind one of our thoughts for the day that I'm particularly fond of: "Grant me the serenity to accept the things I cannot change, the courage to change the things I can, and the wisdom to know the difference."

I think one major lesson I've learned in four years with Coach Smith that will stay with me forever is that there are some things you cannot change. Each of us has a certain amount of God-given ability in athletics, the classroom, whatever. We can supplement that ability with desire and hard work. It's important to understand what you cannot change and what you can change. My freshman year, I played maybe two minutes my first few games. I was very discouraged. There were parts of that situation I couldn't change, others I could by working hard on the things Coach wanted to me improve. I can't make myself have the ability of Michael Jordan. All I can do is improve on what God has given Henrik Rodl. If you lose a game, you're disappointed, but after it's over, you can't change the outcome. There's no sense dwelling on it or letting it affect you. What you can hopefully change, though, are the mistakes you made in that game and not make them again. This philosophy has helped me over these years and will stay with me for life.

Scott and Pat Sullivan did their usual excellent job of keeping us loose in the lockerroom before the Kansas game. After we're all dressed and waiting for the coaches to come in, Scott would get a basketball and he and Pat would start throwing it around like they're Harlem Globetrotters. The problem is that they're not as good as the Globetrotters, and there's no telling where the ball would end up. Usually, it bounced off a wall or someone's head. It was good for a few laughs and a diversion.

Coach Smith came in a few minutes before we went out for warmups. He went over a few key points and then said, "If you don't know how to play basketball by now, there's not much time to teach you."

Fortunately, he's taught us pretty well. The Kansas game was a solid, all-around performance. There were no nerves like two years ago in Indianapolis, no long scoring droughts that killed us then. We got out of the blocks well, withstood a little run by Kansas midway through the first half, then maintained a lead the rest of the game. Donald hit a big 3-pointer with us leading by three and 2:43 left in

Heels Zone In On Michigan.

Carolina learned a zone defense could be fairly effective against Michigan in Hawaii, when the Wolverines claimed a 79-78 win in the Rainbow Classic last December. The defense could jam up Chris Webber and Juwan Howard, and the Wolverines aren't a particularly strong outside shooting team.

The Tar Heels went to the zone frequently in the second half and particularly in the latter stages of the championship game in New Orleans. Several Carolina players felt the defense performed well, particularly considering Michigan connected on only five of 15 three-pointers.

"The zone was very effective for us in Hawaii," Eric Montross said after the 77-71 NCAA title win. "We figured with our improvement on it over the year and because they didn't have a lot of outside shooting, we could kind of pack it in around Webber and Howard. And obviously, Webber."

"I think the zone was very effective," Kevin Salvadori said. "It was someting we learned they were bothered by in Hawaii. We kept putting it on them. A couple of times they got some easy baskets. But for the most part, I thought it worked out well for us.

"There was no stopping Webber one-on-one. We had to either play zone and have everybody jam back and help out or play man-to-man and really jam in and help out. He was really unstoppable, a great player."

Derrick Phelps launches shot over Michigan's Jalen Rose (5) and Juwan Howard (25) during first half of final game.

the game. That shot lifted the margin to six points, 71-65, and that was the key basket. The final was Carolina 78, Kansas 68.

Afterward we dressed and watched the first half of the Michigan-Kentucky game in some seats designated for us behind media row. That was one of the few times we were able to relax a little and have fun. We turned around and waved to our families and friends in the stands. Then at halftime, we went back to the lockerroom and got our bags to leave. We had to walk from one end of the Superdome floor to the other, passing behind the team benches and in front of the temporary stands erected on the floor. All the Carolina fans on the far side saw us leaving and gave us a standing ovation. That was worth a few goosebumps.

Leaving the Superdome to go have dinner, we had no strong feelings about who we'd like to play Monday night in the championship game. But once Michigan won the second semifinal in overtime, I guess there was a consensus of satisfaction with the matchup. We'd shown in Hawaii we were as solid as Michigan, and everyone relished the opportunity to play them again.

Coach Smith did a classy thing Sunday before we went to the Superdome for practice and a press conference. NCAA officials had asked each coach to bring his five starters to the press conference, but Coach said he'd like for Pat Sullivan, Kevin and myself to go as well. We've played eight players pretty consistently all year, and Coach was kind of making a statement that a team doesn't get to the

championship game with just five players. We should have taken all 15 players.

Monday was absolutely miserable. Few of us slept well on the eve of the biggest game of our lives, and the minutes crept by. We had a shoot-around at the Superdome and a team meeting, but otherwise tried to kill time by watching ESPN or movies in our room. You'd look at your watch and it would say "2:25." You'd look again after what seemed like an hour and it would say "2:42."

We went downstairs for our pregame meal at 5 p.m. Coach Guthridge passed around the gold scissors that a fan had sent. Engraved on them was, "North Carolina, 1993 NCAA Champions." That was kind of neat. We passed the scissors around, hoping that we'd be using them later that night.

When we got on the bus a little while later, a lump welled up in my throat when I saw all the parents standing around the bus, waving pom-poms and hugging everyone as they passed by. The Montrosses, the Salvadoris, the Cherrys, Derrick's parents and his little brother, everyone else—there was something about the sight that was very moving. I guess it hit me how much our team touched and affected so many peoples' lives.

Finally, 8 o'clock arrived and it was time to play. The game, of course, was a classic, full of streaks by both teams, marvelous individual plays, interesting strategy by the coaches. The only thing that detracted from the championship atmosphere was that the Superdome is so huge and the crowd so far

Button-Down UNC, Ribald U-M Interesting Match.

The North Carolina players had just left the news conference, victorious again. They'd politely answered everything, revealed nothing. When it was over, they walked stiffly and quickly, all in a line, following their coach.

The Michigan players now entered the room, swaying and smiling, 10 minutes late. Some moved to the beat of rap music through headphones. Chris Webber held a camcorder. Coach Steve Fisher sat on stage, waiting patiently.

"Yo, what's up, Fish?" Ray Jackson hollered as he took a seat next to his coach, in front of 500 media people, many of whom must have wondered the same thing:

How could these two teams, these two coaches, these two styles, reach the same place at the same time, eyeing the same prize?

Not since Kennedy met Nixon have such distinct foes competed on such a large stage. North Carolina (33-4) toes the company line; U-M (31-4) toes the party line. The Tar

Heels button down and clam up. The Wolverines engage and entertain, just as they did Sunday, offering quips on everything from their bald heads to their ribald style.

This is not to say Fisher's permissive manner is any better or worse than Dean Smith's regimentation. It's just different. Way different. And tonight in the Superdome, one style will collect one more national title.

"I'll probably get in trouble for anything I say on this," Tar Heel center Eric Montross said, "but I guess people see this as Squeaky Clean vs. the Bad Boys. Coach Smith doesn't settle for anything less than perfect. We have to be clean-shaven, we have to wear suits and ties. It's the classy image Coach Smith wants, which doesn't mean Michigan isn't classy."

No, just different. The Tar Heels wait their turn, hold their tongues, stand in line. The Wolverines demand their turn, wag their tongues, cut in line.

Bob Wojnowski
The Detroit Free Press, Monday, April 5

Carolina bench explodes after walking violation went unnoticed in the last minute of championship game; Chris Webber made up for that, though, by calling a timeout the Wolverines didn't have with 11 seconds to play.

removed from the playing floor that the crowd is a non-factor. It's not like a lot of ACC games where our crowd or an opposing crowd on the road can be a real part of the game.

Thirty-one minutes into the game, Michigan took a 60-58 lead on a dunk by Chris Webber. Then Donald Williams went to work for us. Twenty-three footer from the left—swish. Twelve-footer on the baseline—swish. Twenty-two footer on the right—boom. Then Derrick made a layup off an assist from Brian and, with 3:07 to play, we were up by one, 68-67.

A lot of talk after the game centered on Coach moving so many players in and out of the game and having his "scorers" on the bench during key periods. A lot of that had to do with people being tired and taking themselves out.

One time he took Donald out and put me in because the two-man was to make the inbounds pass, and since I'm quite a bit taller than Donald, I would be less susceptible to pressure. Donald took himself out a couple of times, and I think he was still a little weak because he'd missed two days of practice with the flu earlier that week. Eric, Pat, Kevin, Scott and I played for one offensive possession following a timeout, that to give the starters an extra minute of rest. The TV people questioned the strategy, and the move appeared not to work well because we didn't get a good shot and I wound up having to take a baseline jumper, off-balance at the buzzer. But on the previous defensive play, all of our guys were bending over at the waist and none of their knees were bent—two sure signs of exhaustion. It was a calculated move by Coach that didn't result in points, but it gave the starters an important extra minute of rest.

George made a super turnaround jumper in the lane and then a wonderful pass out of a trap to Eric, who broke free for a dunk. Those baskets gave us a 72-67 lead, but Michigan cut it back to one with two baskets. Then Pat was fouled and went to the line with a 1-and-1. There's practically no one on the team I feel more comfortable shooting foul shots in that situation, and Pat made one of them to set up the game's most talked-about moment.

Too much attention has been made of Webber's timeout call that resulted in a technical. Too many people have blamed him for the loss. That's ridiculous. One, Webber walked at the other end, so we should have had the ball anyway. That's not open for debate; the violation is clear as crystal on tape. Two, he was surrounded by Derrick and George, who weren't letting him go anywhere. Three, Donald still had to make the foul shots. And four, without Webber, Michigan's not in the game anyway. At times, we couldn't stop him.

So the spotlight was on Donald those last few seconds, and he swished four foul shots to give us the championship, 77-71.

I was proud of Donald Williams and his performance. I can't deny it was sometimes a struggle, losing my starting position midway through the season. But I realize my strengths are passing and defense, and Donald's is scoring. We needed a scorer in there more, and Donald's pretty dang good. I think the competition for minutes with Hubert Davis the previous year sometimes strained our relationship, and I wanted to make sure the same thing didn't happen with Donald.

I'll never forget after an exhibition game in November against High Five America watching Donald, after he had a great game and scored 21 points, come out of the dressing room, see his mother and go over and hug her. Donald had some rough times his freshman year, and seeing him fight through all that and survive and then see him and his mother like that made me get teary-eyed right there.

When the gun sounded, all I can remember was wanting to find everyone on the team and give them a big hug. We'd become such good friends. We'd worked so hard. We'd been in the spotlight for so long. It was such a relief, I can't begin to describe it. I remember being very, very thankful there wasn't another game to play, that there wasn't a championship for the universe or galaxy still to win.

I spotted Susan in the stands and waved to her. She's been great support and definitely the most important person in my life the last few years. I met Susan in 1986 when I was an exchange student at Chapel Hill High. We began seeing each other and then kept our relationship going during the two years I had to return to Germany. We were married in 1991. The following week at the team's awards banquet, I knew I'd get choked up talking about Susan and, sure enough, I did.

One of the special moments of the win was when the team, coaches and managers returned to the lockerroom and we had a few minutes to ourselves—after the celebration on-court and before the press came in. We said our prayer and hugged one another, more out of love this time than the celebratory hugs out on the court. Someone—Coach Guthridge, I think—had written on the chalkboard, "Congratulations. You are a great team. No practice tomorrow."

We were amazed at the crowd gathered at the hotel. The lobby was wall-to-wall people. Everyone wanted to give us a high-five, but all our hands were carrying our bags. I think a few high-fives landed on our heads.

Most of us went down to Bourbon Street. What an atmosphere. Carolina fans

Dome On The Bayou Heels' Home Away From Home.

Who says the Dean Dome is in Chapel Hill?

Geographically, maybe.

But today, in Tar Heel hearts, on Tar Heel maps, it's sitting right here on Poydras Street, a giant mushroom the coach of the NCAA champions would like to paint Carolina blue, tuck into the pocket of his double-breasted suit and take home.

It's sort of spooky, really. You sat there in the Superdome on Monday night, wondering if 62-year-old Dean E. Smith has some sort of New Orleans voodoo going for him.

Eleven years ago, you might remember, after a freshman named Michael Jordan sank a jump shot to give his team a one-point lead over Georgetown with time running out, the Hoyas lost a chance to pull it out when Fred Brown threw the ball to a Tar Heel named James Worthy.

Dean Smith had won his first NCAA championship.

Eleven years later, with his team leading Michigan, 73-71, there was Dean Smith sitting on the same bench inside the Superdome and there went Chris Webber of the Wolverines pulling a Fred Brown, in this case, grabbing a rebound, bringing the ball down, and, horror of horrors, calling a timeout when Michigan had none left.

Technical foul.

Now are you ready for this?

Eleven years later, with exactly 11 seconds left on the

Smith, flanked by Phil Ford and Bill Guthridge, wins Superdome title No. 2.

clock, there stood Donald Williams at the free-throw line, burying Wolverine dreams with two free throws.

And there sat Smith, with his 774th coaching victory and second national championship.

"OK, guys," said Deano, "you can cut down the nets."

So what do you say?

You can say time definitely ran out on the Fab Five. You can say Webber and Brown will be forever linked in Carolina lore. More than anything, you can say the Tar Heels' 77-71 victory reflected the touch of a coach who'd rather be remembered as a teacher.

Peter Finney, The Times-Picayune
Tuesday, April 6

everywhere—dancing, screaming, celebrating. I saw John Kirks, my teammate from Chapel Hill. We'd won the state championship together, and to see him after winning the national championship in New Orleans was very special. We stayed for an hour or so, but after a while it was too much and Susan and I went back to the hotel. I called my parents at work. It was about 9 a.m., their time. My father had gone to watch the game with some friends who had Armed Forces Television. My mother felt she needed to stay home and sleep, but she couldn't sleep so she listened to Armed Forces Radio. She'd stayed up all night but said she wasn't tired at all.

Some of the guys never went to sleep that night. You could see how they looked when we got on the bus to go to the airport Tuesday morning. We all needed a few hours' quiet time on the plane to get ready for the homecoming

celebration in Chapel Hill.

When the bus drove into Chapel Hill, I became overwhelmed with emotion. We went down Franklin Street on the way to the Smith Center, and people were waving and laughing and yelling. You could see some splashes of blue paint from the celebration the night before.

It had been some journey—from learning about Carolina basketball from Roy Williams so many years ago to winning a national championship in New Orleans.

It dawned on me in the season's aftermath, as I planned my return to my native Germany, that I am indeed a rich man through the friends I've made and lessons I've learned from my years at Carolina. ∎

"Senior Scrapbook" chapters by Travis Stephenson, Matt Wenstrom, Scott Cherry and Henrik Rodl edited by Lee Pace.

George Lynch's forte as a Tar Heel was rebounding—1,097 for his career and 10 in this game at Florida State in February.

DAVID E. KLUTHO/SPORTS ILLUSTRATED

Heels' No. 1 Banner: It Will Hang Forever.

BY GEORGE LYNCH

I have always thought that all Carolina basketball teams over the years have had the talent and the confidence to win the national championship. Each team has had a great coach who would give his

players the opportunity to win. This year, it was just a matter of us going out, executing Coach Smith's philosophy and having a little bit of luck along the way. When all of those things happen, Carolina teams are usually very tough to beat. This year, it just

Please turn to Page 54

There are four things you can do with a mistake: Recognize it, admit it, learn from it and forget it.

seemed like everything fell into place.

I'll never forget the feeling I had a few hours after the championship game in New Orleans. The whole team went to Bourbon Street to celebrate, but it was really hectic down there and we got separated pretty quickly. I went back to the team hotel kind of early, but it was impossible to get to sleep. We had just won the national championship, and Donald Williams and I were supposed to appear on the *Good Morning America* show early the next day. (Donald never quite made it, but that's another story altogether!)

My body was very tired, but for some reason I kept thinking that I was going to miss something if I went to sleep. I tried to catch *SportsCenter* on ESPN to see the highlights of the Michigan game, but I couldn't really focus

---

Senior Lynch-Pin Ties Tar Heels Together.

George Lynch was one of the best ever to wear Carolina blue. He proved it in workmanlike fashion in every aspect of the game.

A native of Roanoke, Va., Lynch won award after award in leading Carolina to the NCAA title his senior year, including All-ACC and MVP of the East Regional.

His career totals are amazing: 1,747 points (12.5 per game), 1,097 rebounds (7.8), 241 steals and 233 assists. He's the second all-time leading rebounder in Carolina history, behind Sam Perkins's 1,167.

His seven steals against Florida State on Jan. 27 made him the all-time Tar Heel leader in steals. He and Duke's Christian Laettner are the only two players in ACC history to have had at least 1,500 points, 1,000 rebounds, 200 steals and 200 assists.

Lynch's career was aptly summed up by Coach Dean Smith at the Tar Heels' annual awards banquet in April. His voice cracking, Smith ended his talk by saying, "Believe me, he comes to play every day, every day. If you have that as a coach, you're awful lucky."

Lynch graduated with a degree in Afro-American Studies.

---

on the screen because so many things were running through my mind. I couldn't believe that my college basketball career was over, and I couldn't believe it ended exactly the way I hoped and dreamed it would. I'll never forget this season, and I'll never forget this team.

All year long, from the first pickup games last summer through the final seconds of the championship game, we had confidence that each player would step up and do his part. Everyone came to play, and on most nights we had enough guys playing well to make us a very difficult team to beat. With the guys we had, it was hard not to be confident. On any given night, we had eight or nine guys who could step up and have a big game.

We had Eric Montross, one of the top post players in the country, who was definitely a force inside. We had Derrick Phelps, who could stop any guard in the nation. We had Donald

---

Williams, who could shoot with any guard. We had Brian Reese, who was probably one of the best wing men going one-on-one. Kevin Salvadori was an excellent shot-blocker and defender. Henrik Rödl was a very good shooter and passer. Pat Sullivan was a tough rebounder and shooter. Matt Wenstrom and Scott Cherry played very well in their roles, too. It was really unbelievable to look up and down our roster and see so many people able to do so many things well.

Of course, everyone knows Carolina always has talented players. The key this season was to use all of that talent in the most productive way. When you come to Carolina, it takes awhile to understand Coach Smith's philosophy and to appreciate the fact that there's a reason for everything he does.

My freshman year, we played a lot of juniors and seniors who understood the way Coach Smith looked at the game, and they were given a lot of freedom on the court. My sophomore year, the year we went to the Final Four, we had three seniors (King Rice, Rick Fox, Pete Chilcutt) but we had a "red light-green light" shooting system because everybody else was very inexperienced. That year, a good shot for some players was a bad shot for Coach Smith, so we played by a different set of rules where the players didn't have as much control.

This year, he gave us a lot more freedom because most of us have been here for three or four years and we understood his philosophy. It may sound strange, but it often takes three years to completely understand what is a good shot and what is not a good shot.

I was even taking bad shots early my senior year. I had a horrible game against Michigan in Hawaii when we lost by one point. I hit only five of 18 field goal attempts, and many weren't very good shots. I took to heart one of our thoughts for the day: "There are four things you can do with a mistake: Recognize it, admit it, learn from it and forget it." I think I did all four with my mistakes in that Michigan game, and that helped me the rest of the season.

It takes a lot of discipline to go out there and think like Coach Smith while you're sweating and competing at the same time, but I think this team did it as well as any I've ever seen. We were very unselfish and we always played together, and I think Coach Smith saw that in us. So he changed the rules a little bit, left it up to us to take the right shots in the right situations and, in a way, allowed us to determine our own destiny.

One of the most amazing things about this team was that, even with all of its talent and competitiveness and freedom, it was so close. We had guys who hardly played who could start for most teams in the country, but nobody complained. We had a common goal—winning the national championship—and we allowed ourselves to have a lot of fun together while pursuing that goal. A lot of us arrived in Chapel Hill at the same time, and we grew up together—living on the hall in Granville Towers, having similar academic responsibilities, spending a lot of time together off the court. We had a lot in common, a lot of the same interests. We shared hard times and good times. Somehow, through it all, we really jelled as a team. In the end, I think all of that time we spent together over the years made it easier for us to play together when things got tough on the court.

I remember one time in the Kansas game, Eric and I really got into it for a second and the television cameras made it look really bad. It was one of those situations where we were both competing hard, and we misunderstood each other for a second or two. One of the Kansas players was dribbling between us, and he had the ball on Eric's side. All season in practice, we learned that the man on the ball side was to try to flick the ball away from the dribbler in that situation. When Eric didn't do it a couple of times in a row, I asked him—in a kind of nasty way—why he wasn't more aggressive.

Then Eric told me he had four fouls and he didn't want to foul out of the game. So the next time down the floor, I apologized to Eric. That's when the cameras showed us with our arms around each other. That was the end of it for us, but I think it proved an important point. Most teams would not have been intense enough to communicate with—or yell at—each other in a key situation like that. At the same time, I don't think most teams would have been close enough to get over that kind of problem as quickly as we did.

In the end, the coaching staff had a lot to do with the way all of our talents and personalities meshed together so well. Coach Bill Guthridge, Coach Phil Ford, Coach Randy Wiel and

Assistant AD Dave Hanners all have that competitive spirit that means a lot during the course of a long and tiring season. Before or after practice, Coach Ford would often challenge one of us to a game of H-O-R-S-E or something just to keep us sharp, to keep us humble and to remind us that he can still play. He likes to point out the fact that he's the one with his No. 12 hanging in the rafters.

Sometimes when we played H-O-R-S-E at the Smith Center, he would first tell me to go stand on the baseline, turn around and look up. Then he'd say, "OK, whose name and number do you see up there?" That was his way of trying to psyche us out, but it was also something the guys really got a kick out of. We laughed about it, but we all knew that being remembered—especially at a school like Carolina—was one of the highest honors you could achieve. We knew that winning the NCAA Tournament would give us that opportunity, and that was our ultimate goal.

Next year, when they have our national championship banner hanging up there, I'm going to come back to play Coach Ford one more time. Before we play, I'm going to make him walk to our corner of the Smith Center, turn around and look up. This time it's going to be me asking, "What do *you* see?" That's

Few college basketball careers end with a smile. But George Lynch's did. There was no other way.

Some fans had fun with Montross, who was seen laughing last.

BOB DONNAN

The Monster Mashed.

You know you've arrived when the press keeps wanting to know if you'll turn pro early.

"I've said a million times, I'm not going anywhere," Eric Montross said after the Tar Heels collected the NCAA title.

"Are you kidding?" asked his father, Scott. "To have another year to learn under Dean Smith and Bill Guthridge, for free?"

Montross brought his 7-foot frame as well as a lot of determination and potential to Chapel Hill in the fall of 1990. Too much was expected of him from the outset, given that he'd excelled at the high-school level, where he was seven inches taller than everyone guarding him.

The transition was a big one.

But with the constant supervision of Smith and Guthridge (the Tar Heel assistant who works with big men) and a year-and-a-half of game experience, Montross began to emerge during the middle of his sophomore year as a force in the middle.

By his junior year, he'd become much more of a complete player. Montross had developed a nice hook shot and counter drop-step. He'd become consistent at the foul line. He could play defense without getting into frequent foul trouble and had perfected his ability to keep opponents off the boards.

"What sets North Carolina apart is Montross," Ohio State Coach Randy Ayers said after Carolina's 84-64 win in December. "No one else has anyone like him."

Montross was named first-team All-ACC and second-team All-America by the Associated Press. He was second in the ACC in field-goal percentage at

61.5—the best for a Tar Heel since Brad Daugherty hit 64.8 in 1985-86. He scored in double figures in 36 games (a UNC single-season record) and averaged 15.8 points and 7.6 rebounds a game. He shot 65 percent in six NCAA Tournament games.

"I didn't realize how much he'd improved until I watched the tape of our 1991 Final Four game against Kansas," Smith said. "He'll be playing his best basketball when he's 28."

Montross's career has been closely followed by his family, despite the distance factor from Indianapolis to Chapel Hill. TV cameras picked up Scott Montross on several occasions during the NCAA Tournament, and announcers made note of the irony of Carolina playing Michigan—the alma mater of both Scott and Janice Montross and Eric's maternal grandfather. Even sister Christine is a Michigan student.

A recorded message at the Ann Arbor room of U-M sophomore Christine Montross noted the tugs of loyalties:

"This is Christine and Julie. We've reached a Final Four celebratory compromise and have gone to paint the town Maize and Carolina Blue."

But there was no doubt who this family was pulling for in New Orleans. "It isn't a problem for myself or my wife," Scott said. "We're true blue."

Which blue?

"If it's anyone else but Carolina, we're 'Go Blue,'" he said. "But we're Tar Heels in this tournament. I'm sure it's a lot harder on Christine. She may have to be a little less vocal in her support for the Tar Heels. But believe me, she's Carolina Blue on this occasion."

Lynch didn't realize Montross had four fouls and apologized for his sharp words in the Kansas game.

HUGH MORTON

The competitive spirit of coaches like Bill Guthridge, Dean Smith and Phil Ford (L-R) bolstered the resolve of Lynch to leave Chapel Hill a winner.

something we'll always tease each other about. But the truth is Coach Ford and the rest of the staff had an important part on this team, too—showing up for practice every day, enthusiastic and ready to work hard. That's the way it is here, and that's the way it should be. Whether you're the head coach, an assistant, a manager, a star player or the last guy on the bench, you know that you played an important role in our success.

As soon as you come into this program you feel like you're part of something important, something unique. You realize that there's a lot of history and pride on the line every time you put on a Carolina uniform. It's like it's your duty—and a privilege at the same time—to try to carry on the tradition that was built here before you. This year, many of the former players called just to encourage us. We talked to Kenny Smith, J.R. Reid, Steve Bucknall, Ranzino Smith and just about all of the guys who played here in the past few years. Everyone wants to keep in touch just to see how you're doing. Sometimes they'd call to give us a few pointers or tell us what to expect at a certain point in the season, but the main thing was just to wish us luck and tell us that they were all pulling for us to have a great season.

It's no joke when people talk about the unique atmosphere that surrounds the Carolina basketball program. The minute you sign a letter of intent to attend the University of North Carolina, you're a part of a big family. When you're not going well, they're all there for you

and willing to help any way they can. The other side of that is when you win, you win for yourself and your team—but you win for the rest of your family, too.

It was a great feeling in the end, watching Coach Smith cut down the nets in New Orleans. He's the man who's held this family together over all these years. Our team had been through some tough times with Coach. We played hard every year I was at Carolina, and we have nothing to be ashamed about, but it was definitely hard watching Duke win those back-to-back national championships. After that, I think Coach Smith and the players all felt it was time for North Carolina to win another national championship. Winning conference championships and regular-season titles was nice, but that's pretty much common ground around here now. It was time for something different, something bigger, and we did it.

Ten years from now, if you look at the history of Carolina basketball or the history of the Final Four, we'll be there. All of us—Scott, Matt, Henrik, Travis Stephenson—the whole crew. The great wins over Arkansas and Cincinnati, and then Kansas and Michigan; they'll all be there forever. When we're sitting back many years from now watching Carolina teams in the future, we'll be able to tell our kids and our grandchildren about the time we were there, about the time we won it all. ∎

This "Senior Scrapbook" by George Lynch was edited by Dave Glenn.

Lynch, Montross battle under boards during NCAA semifinal win over Kansas.

A constant for 32 years on the Carolina sideline: Dean Smith fighting for his team.

Smith, North Carolina Hoops' Eternal Flame.

BY RON GREEN JR.

Dean Smith likes jazz, big band tunes and even some gentle rock music. He appreciates gourmet food, likes osso buco for dinner, is passionate about golf and has studied theology for many years.

He was a leader in the integration movement in Chapel Hill in the early 1960s, made a public service announcement in support of a nuclear freeze several years ago and, though he guards his privacy intensely,

Please turn to Page 62

This article originally appeared in "The Charlotte Observer."

he has made it clear that his political views lean decidedly toward the liberal side.

Last February, he and his wife, Linnea, donated $100,000 to the University of North Carolina, and though he preferred to keep the donation quiet, he agreed to a public announcement in hopes it would spur more gifts to the school.

Thirty-two years after he took the Tar Heel job, Smith is the caretaker of a program that has maintained the glow of success, coming as close

WINNINGEST NCAA DIVISION I MEN'S COACHES OF ALL-TIME BY VICTORIES ENTERING THE 1993-94 SEASON

(Minimum 10 head coaching seasons in NCAA Division I)

	Coach, College(s)	Years	Wins
1.	Adolph Rupp (Kentucky)	41	875
2.	Dean Smith (North Carolina)	32	774
3.	Henry Iba (NW Missouri St., Colorado, Oklahoma St.)	41	767
4.	Ed Diddle (W. Kentucky)	42	759
5.	Phog Allen (Baker, Haskell, Central Missouri State, Kansas)	48	746
6.	Ray Meyer (DePaul)	42	724
7.	John Wooden (UCLA)	29	664
8.	Ralph Miller (Wichita St., Iowa, Oregon St.)	38	657
9.	Marv Harshman (Pacific Lutheran, Wash. St., Washington)	47	642
10.	Norm Sloan (Presbyterian, The Citadel, N.C. State, Florida)	37	627

as any program to being college basketball's eternal flame. He reinforced that notion this year by directing his team to the NCAA championship, Smith's second and the school's third.

Even as Duke has won consecutive national championships and made the Final Four its home away from home, Smith has been able to throw counterpunches against those who suggested North Carolina has been mortally wounded. He's now the second-winningest coach in NCAA Division I basketball history with 774 wins, leaving only Adolph Rupp's 875 victories ahead of him.

Smith, 62, remains the flame within the North Carolina program. The image of him on the sideline, his head cocked forward as he peers out from his under bushy eyebrows while the sound of his nasal instructions stab the air, is the image of an era.

Carolina's continued success hasn't come automatically, however. Twice in the past four seasons, the Tar Heels have lost at least 10 games after going 23 years without double-digit losses, and Duke had become the new emperor of college basketball.

At times there have been hints that perhaps Smith and the Carolina program were heading into the inevitable decline that has so far not materialized.

But the Tar Heels reached the Final Four two years ago, landed a spectacular recruiting class a year earlier and set themselves up to be a powerhouse well into the 1990s.

To do so, Smith and his staff have had to fight off the image of rigid commanders who stifle creativity. Critics charge "the system," a term Smith disdains, limits players. They say the faces change but the system never does.

Smith has also been called petty, manipulative, two-sided and the only man capable of holding Michael Jordan under 20 points a game. But he and the program have charged ahead, adjusting against a perception that nothing ever changes, into a promising but uncertain future.

THE RAP

At various times in Smith's career, there has been an undercurrent of concern about the state of his program. He was burned in effigy when one of his early teams struggled. When David Thompson escaped to N.C. State in the early 1970s and when Duke's remarkable rise coincided with a downturn in Chapel Hill, there were suggestions that Smith was past his prime.

More to the point, critics and even some nervous Carolina fans recently questioned whether Smith could get the kind of players he would need to continue the unprecedented success of the Tar Heels' program.

Could he relate to a new generation of basketball players, many of them trained on the streets? Could he bridge the generation gap from Chuck Taylors to Air Jordans?

"It's different now because they're exposed to so much more, but it's not like all 20-year-olds are different than 20-year-olds were before. There are still some things they have in common," Smith said.

"Every human being is different, but there are still things that a 40-year-old and a 20-year-old are likely to think. That hasn't been a problem."

Still, Kenny Anderson rejected Carolina for Georgia Tech because he didn't want "to be another horse in Dean Smith's stable." Grant Hill wound up at Duke instead of Carolina, as did Christian Laettner. The talent level in Chapel Hill dipped for a time.

Then Smith hit the pavement. He went out and got the class that included Eric Montross, Brian Reese, Pat Sullivan, Derrick Phelps and since-transferred Clifford Rozier, called at the time the greatest recruiting class ever.

"He's not one to dwell on what other people say but, at the same time, human nature causes you to hear those things," said Kansas Coach Roy Williams, a long-time Smith assistant. "The worst thing you can do to Coach Smith is tell him he can't do something."

Still, the Jordan line became as familiar as the North Carolina fight song. As a point of clarification, Jordan did, in fact, average 20 points at North Carolina as a sophomore in 1982-83. As a junior, when he averaged 19.6, the Tar Heels were handed perhaps their most bitter defeat in the 1984 regional final to Indiana, and the legend—or the rap—grew.

"I don't care who has the points. I just want North Carolina to have the most of them," Smith says.

Recruiting rivals told prospects that Carolina's program would inhibit their freedom on the court. Scorers get lost at North Carolina.

That's why no one expected Jerry Stackhouse to commit to the Tar Heels. Stackhouse, the best basketball player this state has produced since Jordan, represented everything that didn't fit in Smith's program. At least, that's what many people thought and said.

He would go to N.C. State or Duke or Florida State or any place but Chapel Hill. Stackhouse heard the Jordan line constantly, and it had a funny effect.

"Why was everybody talking against North Carolina?" Stackhouse said. "It wasn't like they were talking against any other school, just Carolina. I thought maybe there's something there that's really good for me.

"I listened to a lot of things. I've heard it all. Some people said they hoped I'd go to North Carolina because that way if they played against me, it would assure them that I'd only score 10 points a game."

The rap. He even heard about it from Smith.

"He more or less brought it up," Stackhouse said. "There were always rumors around that I wasn't interested in North Carolina because I didn't feel I was going to come in and play because freshmen don't play. He said if you're good enough to play, you'll play. I felt like it was the perfect match."

Stackhouse asked about scoring, and Smith had an answer waiting.

"He showed me the statistics," Stackhouse said. "Every year they're among the top-scoring teams in the league. Evidently someone is scoring."

Stackhouse liked the way Smith and the Tar Heels low-keyed their recruiting of him. They didn't bombard him with mail, though Smith would write occasionally.

When they sat down and talked, Smith talked about many things, what mattered and what didn't matter, to him and to Stackhouse. They talked about the NBA, about how much

freshmen get to play, about a wide range of topics.

"When you look at the track record of how their players have done, the trend just goes on," Stackhouse said. "I felt I could come in and, not necessarily follow in their footsteps, but make my own."

THE PERCEPTION

There are certain things Stackhouse and any other player who commits himself to Smith's program must accept. Details are essential. Teamwork is the oxygen of the program.

If there is a guiding principle behind Smith's philosophy, it is the belief that a disciplined man is a free man. Some things never change. Players must be on time. When Smith speaks, everyone listens. Eye contact is important. Players look Smith in the eye when he speaks. Defense is essential. Unselfishness is a virtue.

There is a perception, though, that Smith's coaching philosophy never changes. People call it a system and Smith flinches. A system implies interchangeable parts. That's not how Smith sees his basketball program.

"If someone says you never change, that implies you're not growing. That's a bad sign," Smith said.

In many ways, the program is in constant change. Much of it is private, kept within the invisible confines of the team. Some of it is obvious, like the increased double-teaming by Carolina's defense last season or the emphasis on setting screens to free Hubert Davis the season before.

"People think it's all programmed and computerized, and that's not it at all," Williams said. "People say Coach never changed, that each year it's the same thing. That's hogwash.

"The fundamentals are the same, yeah. But it's the same way at Indiana or anywhere else where one person has had a lot of success. I've heard him say let's change things just for the sake of change."

The past five players to lead North Carolina in scoring have played five different positions. Last year, it was center Eric Montross. The previous year, it was two-guard Hubert Davis. Before that, it was small-forward Rick Fox, power-forward J.R. Reid and point-guard Kenny Smith.

Smith is open to new ideas. At the end of each season, the graduating seniors are called in and asked for suggestions on how to improve any facet of the program.

COMPOSITE ATLANTIC COAST CONFERENCE REGULAR-SEASON STANDINGS FOR THE PAST 27 YEARS (1967-93)			
Team	Won	Lost	Pct.
Carolina	279	87	.762
Florida State	23	9	.719
Duke	199	165	.547
N.C. State	190	176	.519
Virginia	173	193	.473
Georgia Tech	87	113	.435
Maryland	158	208	.432
Wake Forest	139	227	.380
Clemson	130	236	.355

Note: Florida State joined the ACC prior to the 1991-92 season; Georgia Tech joined the ACC prior to the 1979-80 season.

UNIVERSITY OF NORTH CAROLINA
TAR HEELS 70-71 BASKETBALL BLUEBOOK

Smith and assistants Bill Guthridge and John Lotz addressed the team for the cover of the Tar Heels' 1970-71 "Bluebook."

of my favorites.' I never would have thought that," the associate said.

When it comes to basketball, though, nothing is unexpected. Every detail is covered, even if it seems picky or quirky.

"There's a purpose to everything," said former Tar Heel Matt Doherty, now an assistant coach at Kansas. "You're not, as your mother might say, just doing it for your health."

At the top of the daily practice plan are three things that must be committed to memory. Two are basic to the game, an offensive and defensive emphasis of the day. Often it's something as basic as a reminder to catch the ball with two hands.

The third element is the thought for the day, a personal favorite of Smith's, and is usually unrelated to basketball. It is often motivational and always thought provoking, such as:

• "The rewards for those who persevere far exceed the pain that must precede the victory;"

• Or, "Chance favors the prepared mind."

The passage may come from a civil rights leader, a philosopher, a theologian, or from anyplace Smith finds an idea that strikes him.

"I call that using the power of coaching. It gets you thinking," said Smith, who sees himself primarily as a teacher whose reach exceeds the boundary of the basketball court.

THE PREPARATION

Practices are planned daily by the staff, and the plans are filed. If Smith wants to see a practice plan from 1970, it could be found.

"If we have a problem in a particular area, I can look back and see what we were doing another time. Maybe we were spending more time on something," Smith said.

The daily practice plan is broken down to the minute. After pre-practice work on individual skills at several stations at the Smith Center, Smith will blow his whistle to start practice. For the next two hours or so, everything is scheduled, with Smith spending the bulk of his time concentrating on defense. Even two-minute water breaks are worked into schedule.

A byproduct of Smith's attention to detail is an unfailing confidence in him when the game's on the line. Carolina has built a history of spectacular comebacks, including the eight-point rally in 17 seconds against Duke in 1974 through the 21-point second-half rally against Florida State last season. During Carolina's 22-

He also has an annual meeting with his staff, Williams, South Carolina Coach Eddie Fogler, Larry Brown and others, where they critique each other's teams, analyze trends and spend hours watching videotape. Smith or another coach will present a play or a defense and ask the others to shoot it down. The foundation doesn't change but everything else remains in motion.

THE DETAILS

When Smith got into coaching more than 30 years ago, he told himself he didn't want any surprises.

He still produces some, however. An associate of Smith's was shocked recently when he was in a car with the coach as an oldies radio station played softly in the background.

"A song came on, something like, 'Crimson and Clover,' and he said, 'Turn it up. That's one

Future Tar Heels Jeff McInnis (L), Jerry Stackhouse watch from behind Smith in Tar Heels' win over Duke March 7.

point comeback against Wake Forest in 1992, Smith told his team how big its deficit would be at each timeout. "He was right every time," said Hubert Davis.

Practice is closed to outsiders except those who receive Smith's written permission to attend. Guests receive a blue index card that is picked up by a manager when practice starts. Guests are asked to sit in the first four rows of the upper deck in the Smith Center on the side facing where the team benches would be during games.

The managers chart practice. They know who got offensive rebounds, who got loose balls, who hit how many shots and from where.

"You need objective stats to support what you see," Smith said. "I may think a guy isn't shooting well. That's subjective. But I can ask a manager how he's shot the last 700 shots and he'll tell me 56 percent. My subjective part was wrong."

To keep the competitive edge, managers keep track of which side wins in each set of practice drills. If the white team beats the blue team easily in a session concentrating on halfcourt zone offense, the losers run sprints.

There is also a points system that rewards players for a variety of things, such as diving for loose balls and setting screens. From the players' point of view, points can be cashed in to avoid running. From the coaches' angle, it helps build habits that pay off in games.

The attention to detail carries over to pregame warmups. Managers keep track of missed layups before the game. During the pregame shoot-around, there's a plan. Players have partners and divide their time between shooting and rebounding. Managers call out six rotations during the shoot-around.

It goes all the way down to the warmup jackets the Tar Heels wear. Those stylish jean jackets Alexander Julian designed stay on for five minutes during pregame. They are taken off by the entire team at the same time.

During games, assistant coaches chart everything from timeouts to points per possession. Official stat sheets reveal one set of numbers. North Carolina's ("The way we keep them," Smith likes to say) often reveal another.

In Carolina's statistics, for example, players get credit for assists if their teammate gets fouled attempting a field goal. That wouldn't be counted on the official stats.

All the numbers are tabulated and awards given after each game. On a wall in the North Carolina locker room is a chart listing game-by-game winners in eight categories: defensive award, assist-error ratio, offensive rebounds, drawn charges, screener award, good players award (first to loose balls, savvy, etc.), blocked shots and deflections.

THE IMPACT

It is all part of a process that Smith sees as bigger than basketball.

"No one is above the system. That's a proven fact," Jordan said.

It doesn't work for everybody. Rozier, part of Smith's now-famous recruiting class three years ago, decided to leave the program and transfer to Louisville after his freshman year. In an interview after his transfer, Rozier said, "Coach Smith is a militant coach. He's a disciplinarian. He's like a sergeant in the army. He teaches you and makes you learn."

Some habits are hard to break. That's why freshmen often struggle under Smith. Old habits must be replaced by new habits. In building habits, Smith is building discipline. In building that discipline, he believes, he is building a freedom on the basketball court.

"There is a concern that he doesn't let this team go enough, doesn't let them play freely enough," said sports psychologist Dr. Bob Rotella of the University of Virginia, who has watched Smith's teams for more than 20 years. "It's a problem in that disciplined a system if you never let them go. But it works as long as you let them go at a certain point. You've got to say, 'Okay guys, you've got it. Now go put it to work.'

"It's a lot like bringing up children. When they turn 18, you tell them, 'We've brought you up. Now it's time to go live your life.'"

THE FUTURE

Dean Smith despises talk about coaching records. As the victories have continued to pile up, he has brushed off questions about each milestone.

But the question of his future and the possibility of breaking Adolph Rupp's record of 875 victories, which could happen by 1997, won't go away.

Smith has insisted he won't break Rupp's mark. He said once he would retire first, even if it meant stepping down when he was one victory shy. Asked about that comment recently, Smith said, "I'd say the same thing again ... I have no intention of (breaking it)."

Others believe he will be swayed by those close to him, particularly his former players, for whom the record would carry a special meaning. Records are a byproduct of his success.

"I think he really enjoys coaching," said Bill Guthridge, Smith's assistant of 26 seasons. "I think he'll coach a long time."

Only Smith may know when the flame goes out. ■

NCAA DIVISION I ALL-TIME WINS BY SCHOOL	
CAROLINA	1,570
Kentucky	1,561
Kansas	1,515
St. John's	1,482
Duke	1,435
Oregon St.	1,415
Temple	1,393
Notre Dame	1,362
Pennsylvania	1,362
Syracuse	1,360

A TEAM
FOR THE AGES

The 1993 Tar Heels were a team comprised of an intelligent and savvy point guard, a prolific shooter, an athletic and explosive small forward, an omnipotent and possessed power forward and an experienced and dominating center. There were a host of complementary players who added the crucial blocked shot, steal, assist or baseline jumper when needed. The result was simply the best team in the country.

THE 1993 NCAA CHAMPIONS

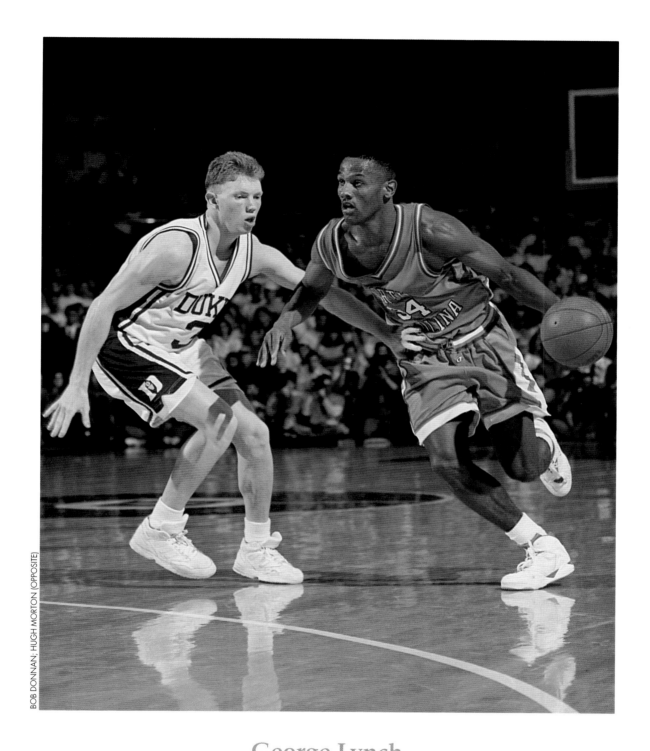

George Lynch
*was Mr. Everything for the Heels: rebounding,
scoring, passing, defense and leadership.*

Eric Montross
was a force under the basket no one could stop—
whether he was feathering a hook or slamming a dunk.

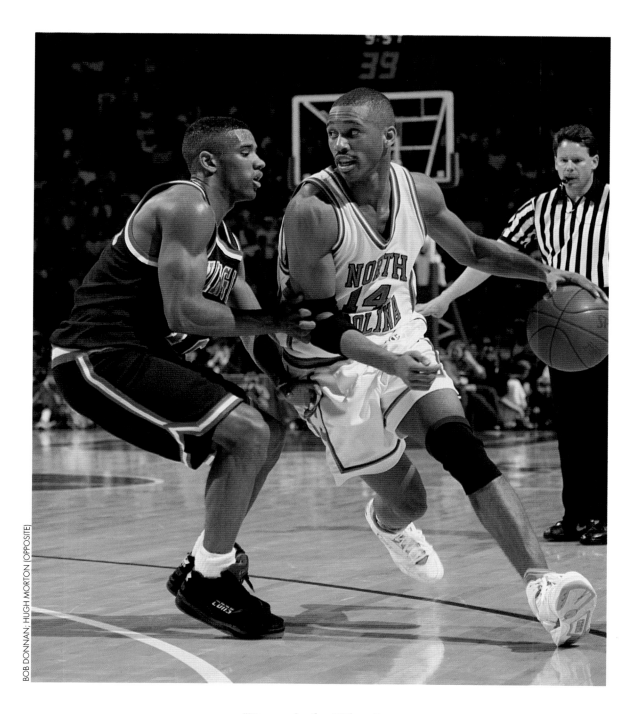

Derrick Phelps

*was in someone's face or by his man in the blink
of an eye as he made the Heels' attack click.*

MARK DOLEJS/THE HERALD-SUN; DAVID KLUTHO/SPORTS ILLUSTRATED (OPPOSITE)

Brian Reese

*detonated in midseason, offering an explosive move to
the hoop and great leaping ability under the boards.*

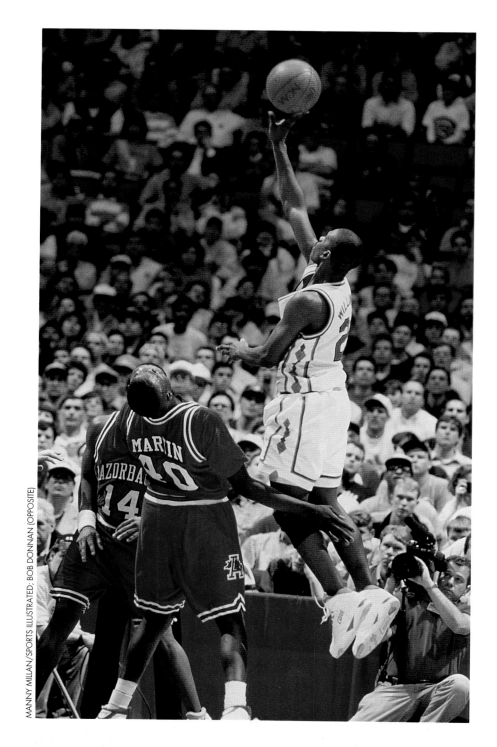

Donald Williams
*carved his niche in Carolina basketball history
by knifing foe after foe with a silken jump shot.*

The Aftermath
included a jovial net-cutting ceremony, a frenzy of support back in Chapel Hill after the team's return from New Orleans, a trip to the White House and a first ball thrown by Dean Smith at Yankee Stadium. The Tar Heel coach subbed for the previously scheduled Jim Valvano, whose illness kept him at home and caused his death several weeks later.

Same view, 11 years apart: Noted Carolina alumnus Hugh Morton captured these nearly identical images in 1982 and 1993 of Dean Smith directing the Heels in the final minutes of NCAA championship games in the Superdome.

'82 Fab Five Rumor Titillates Tar Heelia.

By ART CHANSKY

Like the wave rhythmically moving around a sold-out stadium, the word circulated the giant ballroom of the Hotel Inter-Continental, where the pre-game pep rally was about to begin.

Did you hear? Michael's meeting with the team.

Jean Durham, Woody's wife, was the first to catch wind of the chilling news. "I knew something was up when Woody called Coach Smith to do his pre-game radio show," she said, "and Linda told him it would

Please turn to Page 82

have to be moved back a half hour."

Linda Woods is Dean Smith's secretary. She schedules his appointments and confirms his rituals. The pre-game radio show is usually taped four hours before tipoff. So when Linda said it would have to be moved closer to the start of the NCAA championship game against Michigan, Jean Durham mixed her information with her imagination.

"Can you picture that," she said, "Michael telling the team about 1982. It gives me goosebumps."

The story was to get even more tingly. Not only was Michael Jordan talking to the Tar Heels before the biggest game of their lives, *all* five starters from the '82 national champs were with him, and them, at that very moment.

As more people heard it, the rumor became gospel.

After all, Matt Doherty and Jimmy Black were already in New Orleans. Doherty, a Kansas assistant coach, remained after the Jayhawks were beaten by Carolina in Saturday's semifinals. And Black, the plucky point guard now on the Notre Dame staff, was in town for the annual coaches' convention.

Jean Durham asked around to confirm what she had just heard—the juiciest part of the story. "I know the Bulls aren't playing tonight, but what about the Lakers and Seattle?"

There were no NBA games tonight, she was told. Everybody's off.

That made the blockbuster news even more believable.

Jordan had not only flown into New Orleans on the private jet he leases, he had first gone out to the West Coast to pick up James Worthy and Sam Perkins. They were all together again, meeting with the Tar Heels, as the story rampaged its way through the ballroom.

The story still stands the hair straight up for those who hear it, even untrue. In fact, only Doherty and Black were in New Orleans—both attended the game—while Worthy, Perkins and No. 23 watched on television from far away. Nobody but the coaches talked to the team before the game, although Jordan did go public with a prediction: Carolina by six.

***

Only the Carolina basketball phenomenon—and family—could concoct such a spine-tingling tale, one that slammed-dunked another rumor that President Bill Clinton was coming, too. No contest.

In fact, there were those in the ballroom who knew it not to be true but still passed the story on so others could share in the sensation. If not the team, it sure got the crowd pumped.

And why not? The tie between Carolina and its former Tar Heels, from Austin to Zaliagiris,

is legendary. Weren't Barlow, Bell, Bunting, Clark, Doughton, Kupchak, Kenny Smith, Shaffer, Scott, Miller, O'Donnell, Vinroot and Waddell among many of the more than 200 lettermen under Dean Smith who showed in the Big Easy?

Players graduate but they don't really leave. They just live and work somewhere else until they can go back, or meet up, for games their successors now play. Thus, it made perfect sense for Carolina's "Fab Five" of '82 to come on down, although the sight of Jordan might have caused a scene even New Orleans couldn't handle.

Lesley Visser of CBS heard that Jordan was coming to the game, and she spent much of that afternoon trying to track him down. Rick Brewer, Carolina's sports information director, assured her that, indeed, Jordan was not entering the building. "His parents are here, and they'll be sitting with Kenny Smith," Brewer told her, "but there's no way Michael could come here without getting mobbed."

Logic or logistics had no place this night. It was a story no one would disbelieve, one all Carolina fans wanted to squeeze and hold onto until the final buzzer sounded and their champions had again conquered the world of college basketball.

So, after the pep band struck up its tried and true refrains—including an appearance from the NCAA-banned Blues Brothers—and the cheerleaders had 'em shakin' the chandeliers, Carolina's crowd headed for the Superdome higher than a Jordan jam.

Somehow, they knew lightning was about to strike again in New Orleans, and there would be another party around midnight down on Bourbon Street.

***

On Saturday morning, about eight hours before the NCAA semifinals, Scott Montross was sitting in the newly named Tar Heel Pub at the Inter-Continental, ready to be interviewed by WCHL radio back to Chapel Hill. He was wearing a warm-up suit, which he had put on after his morning jog with Carolina Assistant Coach Bill Guthridge.

Montross and Guthridge often run together before games at home and on the road. As Dean Smith's chief aide of 26 years, Guthridge *has* to be at every game; Montross just chooses to hopscotch the country with his wife Janice to see their son Eric move some bodies around in the paint.

Scott Montross saw 30 of Carolina's 38 games in person, and his wife actually witnessed 31. Scott missed the trip to Florida State because he had committed to a cross-country ski race in the wilds of Minnesota,

Roy Williams, Dean Smith, Bill
Guthridge share laugh before
Kansas game; but there were no
smiles for Williams or assistant Matt
Doherty as the clock wound down.

MARK DOLEJS/THE HERALD-SUN; HUGH MORTON (INSET)

where he finally found a bar with a satellite dish. He made it for the second half and had to pay the bartender $20 to keep from switching to ice fishing.

In New Orleans, Montross and Guthridge ran by themselves along the Mississippi River, turning down an invitation to join Kansas Coach Roy Williams and Oregon Coach Jerry Green. All four had run together two years

Calendar Boy Williams Makes Big Time.

Roy Williams was the No. 3 assistant on the Tar Heel staff for eight seasons from 1979-86, before Eddie Fogler left the staff and Williams was elevated to "full-time, full-pay."

During that period, he did a number of odd jobs to make money beyond what he could earn in salary—speaking at camps, delivering tapes of Carolina coaches' TV shows to statewide TV stations, to mention two odd jobs.

Williams talked at a Final Four press conference of the dire straights his family was in financially early on.

"My wife and children wanted to eat," he said, so he developed an annual Carolina basketball calendar that helped supplement his income.

Williams created a poster-sized calendar with all the players' photos and a schedule for the coming year. Williams drove 10,000 miles in 10 weeks the first year and sold 9,000 calendars.

"I'd go see a customer, get on my knees, and ask him to buy 100 calendars," Williams says. "Then I'd put the name of his company across the bottom."

Eventually, Williams refined and improved his business so that he was spending five weeks on the road, driving 5,000 miles and selling over 50,000 calendars.

Williams noted that since the No. 3 assistant is prohibited by today's NCAA rules of receiving more than $16,000 from the university—with no other outside income allowed—he probably wouldn't be where he is today if those rules had been in effect 10 years ago.

before at the Final Four in Indianapolis, when Green was an assistant coach on the Jayhawk team that knocked UNC out in the semis.

It was to be a friendly run, but Guthridge used his dry sense of humor when Williams called. "He said, 'We ran with you last time and you beat us,'" Green related. "'This time we're not going with you.'"

Williams, a part-time assistant on the '82 Tar Heels, had popularized a tradition started 11 years prior, when he and other members of the Carolina party jogged down to the Mississippi and spat in the river. Williams had done it the week before while Kansas was winning the Midwest Regional in St. Louis, and thousands of Jayhawk fans lined a local river in Lawrence, Kan., to huck a collective big one as their team headed for New Orleans.

Guthridge and Montross had left the spitting to Kansas as they ran along the river, and now the father of the nation's best center was trying

to explain the other, more important traditions that sent his son to Chapel Hill. Talking slowly into the microphone, he couldn't quite do it.

"You know, we got interested in the recruiting process and researched all the schools that Eric was looking at," he said. "Most of the visits went the way we expected. We didn't really learn anything new about the other schools or coaches he was considering.

"But then we went to Carolina, and there was something about it that we couldn't put our finger on after visiting with Coach Smith. He didn't paint a perfect picture of what playing college basketball would be.

"He said it was going to be a challenge and that it would be difficult for Eric at first. But he and Bill have done everything they said they would do, and more. Not a single thing has happened that he didn't tell us about."

The Carolina and Montross families make a perfect match. Both have more substance than even their considerable style, traditions that run generationally deep. Dean Smith and his staff aren't afraid to battle the odds when they know Chapel Hill is the best place for a recruit. And in the Montrosses, they found people willing to look beyond the obvious.

Scott Montross played for Michigan on the Cazzie Russell teams of the 1960s and his father-in-law, Jack Townsend, was a two-time All-America for the Wolverines. And as one of the most prominent lawyers in Indianapolis, Scott felt the peer pressure for Eric to stay home and play for Bob Knight.

Both schools finished a distant second to Carolina, which had the more stable program and consistent coach. In the end, the only tie that counted was the immediate family.

His disagreement with Knight over a legal matter is an old story, but one that Scott Montross will share if pressed. And when a TV announcer foolishly asked him whether he'd be rooting for his son or his alma mater Monday night, Montross said simply, "Blood is thicker than anything else."

On Monday night, after the Tar Heels had held off Michigan for the title, Montross took off his Carolina blue sport coat and waved it over his head midway up section 141 in the Superdome. The Michigan man from Indiana was not afraid to tell the world he's a Tar Heel—and proud of it.

***

Sometimes, Dean Smith likes to house his team far from the madding crowd at big games and tournaments. But not this time. Taking a page from 1982, when the Tar Heels stayed at the Monteleone in the French Quarter, Smith accepted the NCAA-designated hotel three blocks from Bourbon Street.

Of the 500 rooms at the Inter-Continental, about 450 were occupied by UNC players, coaches, officials and fans. From morning to evening the lobby was filled with Carolina folks, occasionally divided by tall figures that made up the "Who's Who" or "Who's That?" of Heel hoops.

Even remnants from the McGuire era were there, Kearns and Cunningham and Brennan, to name three. Ex-team managers, maybe the most loyal, were represented by the vaguely familiar faces of Eddie Burke from the '60s, John Barrett from the '70s, Chuck Duckett and Mark Isley from the '80s.

They were all there to see the current Tar Heels, for whom four years must pass faster than for the fans. Not too many seasons from now, it won't be uncommon to see Kevin Salvadori joining his two brothers and father at some, any, Carolina game, anchoring the tallest tailgate party in that town.

So, as the 1993 Tar Heels filed past the throng on the way from the hotel to the team bus, it was easy to wonder whether they realized this was their chance to catch a moonbeam in a jar.

Wearing semi-grim faces, they all looked like *someone* had given them the pep talk of their lives. Only Eric Montross and Dante Calabria flashed thin smiles, Montross because he got the biggest roar and Calabria because, like most freshmen in the Final Four, he couldn't have known how hard it was to get there.

Calabria evoked memories of Mike O'Koren, who as a cocky freshman starred for the 1977 NCAA runners-up and vowed to get his team back to the Final Four and win it all. He never did, as the Tar Heels were knocked out early the next three years. The All-America point guard on two of those O'Koren teams was Assistant Coach Phil Ford, who was going for the net he missed as a player.

Six blocks away, the family was already assembling to live vicariously for the next few hours. To some, it meant even more than to others.

Kenny Smith quarterbacked two of the greatest Tar Heel teams ever. In both 1984 and 1987, Carolina swept through the ACC regular

HUGH MORTON

Phil Ford finally cut down the championship net—16 years after losing the final to Marquette as a junior.

season undefeated (14-0) with Smith at the point and a lineup of NBA futures. Neither team reached the Final Four.

Now an all-pro with the Houston Rockets, Smith took advantage of the night off to catch the one-hour flight to New Orleans. As he walked down the aisle of section 140 in the Superdome, Smith shook hands and signed autographs for fans and friends who remembered his grace on the court as well.

Actually, Smith had been in Tar Heel minds most of the season, as they watched Derrick Phelps take the same kind of spills that marked Smith's career and knocked him out of half his freshman season with a broken wrist.

That was the year he had Jordan on one side, Doherty on the other, Perkins and Brad Daugherty up front. It was also the year Smith played with one and a half hands against an inferior Indiana team that upset Carolina in the Sweet 16. Three years later, after another undefeated regular season with Wolf, Reid,

Lebo and Popson, he ended his college career with a Final Eight loss to Syracuse. So this one was for millionaire Kenny Smith, too.

It was also for Roy Williams, the long-time Carolina disciple whose Kansas team had been taken out by the Tar Heels two days earlier. Williams cried after that loss but soon turned his attention to the final, where the man to whom he owes every professional accomplishment in his life was going after another national championship.

"I hurt for my team," he said after the semifinal defeat, "but come Monday night I'll be pulling hard for North Carolina. If you don't understand that, you don't know anything about Roy Williams."

As Williams and his wife Wanda made their way down section 140, they were treated almost presidentially by the Carolina crowd. Shaking every hand and hugging a few shoulders, Williams was anxious for his mentor to win a second title. He had been by Smith's side when the first monkey was extracted in 1982, and since then he'd heard the cracks about the big ape being back.

About three hours later, Williams was dancing up the same aisle he had come down.

***

No one deserved a dance more than UNC Chancellor Paul Hardin, a good man and courageous leader who was taking a well-needed respite from some important controversies back home. Before he left, the students demanding a free-standing Black Cultural Center on campus had marched to his door several times. Upon his return, they would take over his office before being ousted by police. This weekend, Hardin was, purely and simply, a basketball fan.

While other distinguished university officials feel decorum is part of their demeanor, Hardin has no such inhibitions when it comes to Carolina games. He is often halfway out of his seat, both arms raised high, as a Tar Heel 3-pointer is on the way. He is supportive, vocal and, sometimes, just another frustrated fan.

A Duke graduate who returned to North Carolina in 1988 after serving as president of Drew University, SMU and Wofford during the prior 20 years, Hardin watched respectfully as his alma mater stole the basketball headlines from Carolina. Broken-hearted over the Tar Heels' semifinal loss in 1991, Hardin cheered quietly for Duke as it won the national championship that same weekend.

So, it must not have been lost on Hardin that Duke Coach Mike Krzyzewski was sitting close by on the CBS broadcast platform, commentating on the game his team had played in the last three years. Hardin even

smiled once as the Carolina students, sitting behind the broadcast booth, gave Coach K some good-natured needling before, during and, especially, after the game.

Also in the crowd was Carolina football coach Mack Brown, sitting adjacent to AD John Swofford and his family. Brown, who left Tulane for Chapel Hill in 1988, skipped one day of spring practice to pull for the basketball team and coach he watches closely.

Brown was scheduled to return to New Orleans and the Superdome later that year to meet his old school. What he really coveted—and some day may achieve—was a New Year's Day trip to the Dome for the Sugar Bowl and a shot at his own national championship. On Brown's way out of the cavernous football stadium, more than one well-meaning fan said he'd see Mack back there in 1994.

One section away sat Dean Smith's family and closest friends. Paul Fulton, the former president of Sara Lee and new dean of the UNC Business School, was there, as was Tassie Dempsey. This was the first Final Four, indeed the first NCAA Tournament, she was attending without her beloved husband Jimmie.

After losing him to cancer last summer, Tassie wasn't sure how many trips she'd make from Wilson to Chapel Hill without Jimmie. It was different riding down Route 264 and then I-40 without him, but she didn't miss a single ACC game in the Smith Center. And when the Tar Heels reached New Orleans, Smith made sure Tassie was a member of the travel party.

That's the way it is with Carolina basketball, from the former players who come (and can't come) for various reasons, to the families of the players who become regular fans after their sons graduate. James and Deloris Jordan were there, even though their youngest wouldn't dare to be, and somewhere in the crowd must have been the parents of a future Tar Heel star.

John Grimes, Derrick Phelps' stepfather, probably looks forward to the day when he won't have to wonder if No. 14 is going to get up after a defensive dive or break-away dunk. Clinging to Derrick's mom and their younger son, they also danced their way into the New Orleans night after the nets had been cut down and the tape cut off for the last time.

"Thank God he has the whole summer to rest," Grimes said, smiling and relieved. "We don't know what it will be, but we're gonna wrap Derrick in something for a long time."

Too late. The multitudes who call themselves the Carolina basketball family had already wrapped him in their arms—forever. ■

Art Chansky, a 1970 Carolina graduate, authored "March To The Top" in 1982.

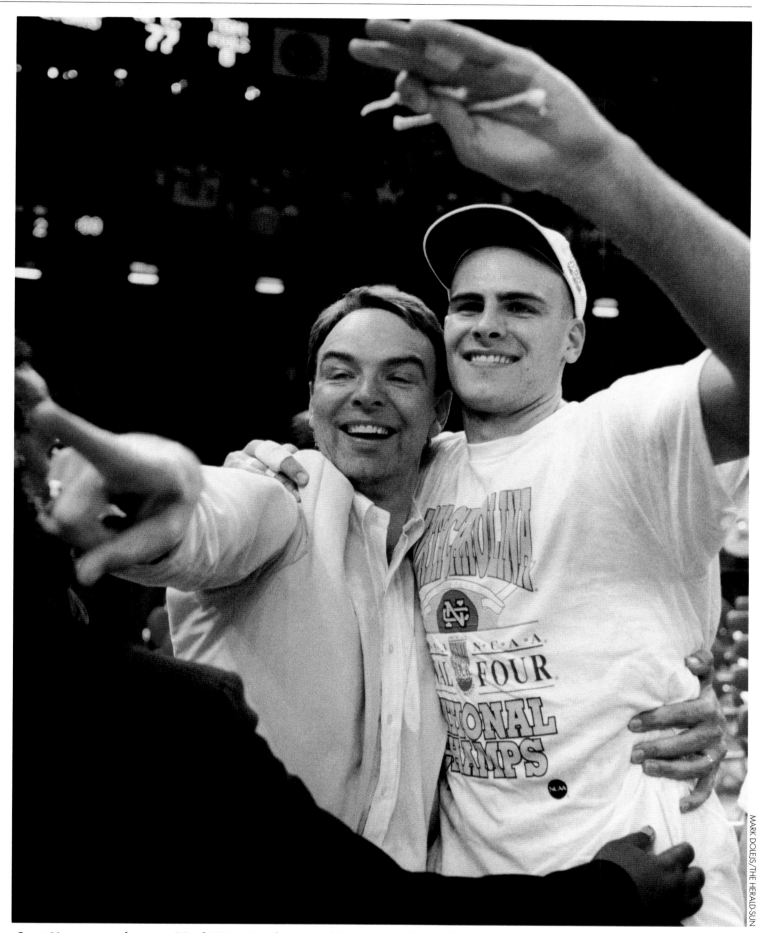

Scott Montross, who saw 30 of 38 Tar Heel games this year, rejoices with son Eric after NCAA final.

'Special' Only Word For Team & Coach.

By RICK BREWER

When I think of the 1992-93 Carolina basketball season, one of the first things I'll remember concerns a football game.

It was the night of December 29 and I was in Atlanta, where the Tar Heels were preparing for their Peach Bowl game with Mississippi State.

Fortunately, our hotel had a "sports bar" where the Carolina-Michigan basketball game in the Rainbow Classic could be seen on big-screen televisions. Even though the Tar Heels were trailing the Wolverines at the half, 40-36, I felt very confident. I was sitting with Jeff Elliott, one of our associate athletic directors, and Mark Maye, a great quarterback here in the 1980s.

As the second half went back and forth, I pointed out this was the kind of game the Tar Heels always seemed to win. And when Michigan called its second and third timeouts within 30 seconds of each other and still 1:37 to go, I couldn't believe it.

"I guess I've watched Dean Smith coach too long," I said. "But I can't believe they've used all their timeouts with so much time left."

A rebound basket by Chris Webber put the Wolverines up 77-76 with 31 seconds to play and Carolina took its first timeout. A play was set up for Donald Williams, who drove into the lane and hit a short jumper. That put Carolina back ahead with only 13 seconds left.

Out of timeouts, Michigan frantically rushed the ball upcourt. Center Juwan Howard nearly turned the ball over at midcourt. The ball finally got to Jimmy King, who had to force up a shot from the right corner. Unfortunately for Carolina, both George Lynch and Eric Montross went out to try and block the shot. With the board uncovered, Michigan's Jalen Rose was able to go over Derrick Phelps, grab the rebound and lay it back in as the buzzer sounded.

"Shows how much I know," I said as we left our table. "In the end, not having a timeout really helped them. If they had called one, Coach would have set his defense differently. They might have still won, but not like that."

***

Just over three months later in New Orleans, I thought about that night after Michigan had again needed a timeout in the final minute of a tight game. The Wolverines had called their last two within a 32-second span and 0:46 still remaining in the national championship game.

With 11 seconds left in a two-point game, Webber was trapped on the sideline by Lynch and Phelps, a place an opponent doesn't want to be when playing North Carolina. Faced with nowhere to go and nearing a five-second call, he asked for the infamous timeout his team did not have.

It's unfortunate for Webber that so much has been written about that play. He had kept his team in the game with a sensational performance.

But as I stood in the pressroom afterward, answering questions of writers, I thought of the man in the dark suit sitting on the Carolina bench who not only knew how many timeouts Michigan had left, but also had told his players they had three fouls to give before Michigan would go to the free throw line.

This is not a condemnation of Michigan Coach Steve Fisher who, in fact, tried to protect his player by taking blame for the timeout mistake. It is instead just another example of why Dean Smith is the best in the country at what he does.

No, Carolina doesn't win every game it plays. And Michael Jordan did play on only one national championship team. And the Tar Heels have won just two NCAA titles in Smith's 32 years as head coach.

But all that only seems to bother fans of other schools and a few cynics in the media. I've never heard a player leave here after three or four years and say he was sorry he had come. That's why those players return to the campus so often, call the basketball office regularly and are fairly successful in whatever they are doing.

Jordan, for example, whom the above-

BOB DONNAN

mentioned critics like to say was "kept under wraps" in Chapel Hill, seems to be doing pretty well for himself. He is one of Smith's biggest fans, except when they're facing each other on the golf course in the summer.

When this season started I can recall a couple of conversations in which writers predicted that Smith would be especially driven this year because of Duke's recent success in the NCAA Tournament. He had too much pride, they said, to take a backseat to what had been accomplished just eight miles away.

These people who felt Smith had an obsession about Duke don't know the man as well as they might like to think. In fact, I felt all season that just the opposite was true—Smith seemed to be as relaxed as ever and having more fun than at any time in years. This was despite the fact Carolina, as usual a preseason Top 10 selection, was playing without its top scorer from 1992, Hubert Davis.

That's not to say Smith wasn't the same competitive man he's been for 32 years. I'm not sure if there's anyone as competitive as he is. But people asked me all season about why he seemed so loose. After a heartbreaking loss to Georgia Tech in the ACC Tournament final, he had writers in the interview room laughing with one-liners.

Inside, I knew he was hurting because he liked this team so much and he was sorry it had failed to reach one of its goals. That's one of the amazing things about the man—win or lose, he has the ability to control his emotions. The same thing goes for game situations. He stays calm under incredible pressure, which has to have a reassuring effect on his players.

During preseason practice I asked him how he did it. I was about to have a meeting which I knew would be very emotional, and I wanted to try to keep control of myself. In typical Smith fashion, he laughed off his own ability. But he did talk to me at length about the problem I was facing. As the season progressed, even during the NCAA Tournament, he would regularly ask me how things were going. He wasn't prying, but simply expressing his genuine concern.

At the same time, he was putting together the best basketball team in the country. This was a special team because it had a very special player — George Lynch.

He put on one of the great performances of the season in a January 24 win over Seton Hall at The Meadowlands. He had 25 points, seven rebounds and three steals. In addition, he limited Jerry Walker to only six shots and 10 points.

Although he somehow wasn't officially credited with an assist, it was a Lynch pass that clinched the 70-66 victory. The Pirates called time out with 28 seconds left after a John Leahy 3-pointer had cut the Tar Heel lead to 68-66. Then, on a perfectly executed inbounds play, Lynch hit Phelps streaking all alone for an uncontested dunk that sealed the win.

As we stood outside the lockerroom afterward, Skip Myslenski, the national college basketball writer for the *Chicago Tribune*, smiled and asked me, "Is George Lynch the best

Eric Montross signs an autograph for a young Tar Heel fan on Bourbon Street Friday night before the semfinals.

JIM BOUNDS/THE NEWS & OBSERVER

unknown player in the country?"

I knew what he meant. There were more heralded players, bigger scorers, but could any of them do all the things Lynch could?

The next game was at home against Florida State and featured an incredible second-half rally which saw Carolina come from 21 points down with less than 12 minutes to play and score an 82-77 victory. Henrik Rodl had three 3-pointers in that rally and Donald Williams had 17 second-half points. But it was Lynch who finally put the Tar Heels ahead with a dunk after he picked off a Charlie Ward crosscourt pass in the backcourt.

It was Lynch who had four straight double-scoring, double-rebounding performances in the East Regional and the Final Four as Carolina drove to the national championship. The last player to finish the NCAA Tournament with four straight double-doubles was Larry Bird in 1979. It was the first time that had been accomplished by a player on a national championship team since 7-foot-4 Tommy Burleson of N.C. State in 1974.

There are other special moments in a special season that stand out in my memory:

* Lynch hitting Williams for a layup off a backdoor play in the East Regional semifinals against Arkansas. Carolina had only a one-point lead and 51 seconds to go. The Razorbacks probably felt the Tar Heels were going to burn some time off the clock, but instead they scored immediately. Then on the other end of the floor, Lynch forced a turnover and Williams hit free throws to clinch the win.

Then, after the game, the team bus was returning to its Manhattan hotel. As the players got off, Lynch noticed one of the city's homeless people standing at the next street corner. He went around the bus and picked up all the leftover sandwiches from the team's post-game snack and put them in a bag. He walked over and handed them to the man without a word, turned and went into his hotel.

It was an act only one or two people saw and wasn't done to get attention anyway. It was simply George Lynch being himself.

* Williams nailing two remarkable 3-pointers against Cincinnati in overtime of the East Final, then hitting 10 of them in New Orleans. He had been a backup point guard as a freshman to become a better ball-handler and to face Phelps every day in practice. If he could play against Phelps, he could play against anyone. Plus, with Hubert Davis around, he wasn't going to get any playing time at the other guard anyway. Then as a sophomore, Smith shifted him to the big guard spot, where he became a key performer during the 34-4 run.

* Brian Reese exploding for 25 points to spark a hard-fought win at Florida State. Reese, after shaking off early-season injuries, became a key factor in Carolina's championship drive. He was sensational in the ACC Tournament, making the All-Tournament team and almost pulling out the game in the final with his 3-pointers.

Then there was "the dunk." Against Cincinnati in the East Final, Carolina had the ball under its own basket in a tie game and 0.8

seconds to go. With Smith drawing up a play and his players executing it perfectly, Reese found himself so wide open under the basket he couldn't believe it. Stunned by how open he was, he missed a dunk which would have ended the game.

* Eric Montross dominating play inside against two 7-footers from Kansas in the national semifinals. As much as that, I will remember and appreciate Montross taking the time in early December to talk to a small boy who thinks Eric is the greatest thing going. Having seen the class he has in so many ways, I know that child is pretty close to being right.

* Sitting by a telephone at the Charlotte Coliseum and waiting anxiously for a call from the hospital on the condition of Phelps after he was severely injured in the ACC Tournament semifinals. It reminded me of two weeks before, when Phil Ford and I were walking through the Tallahassee Airport. We had just arrived there for a game the following day with Florida State. As we passed an open bar with a television on, we both heard the words "World Trade Center."

"What was that guy saying about the World Trade Center?" Ford asked.

"That's all I heard. Are you concerned about all the stocks you own?" I joked, not realizing what had happened in New York that day.

It was only later that we learned the building had been the target of a terrorist attack. It was news that frightened Phelps, whose mother worked there. Fortunately, Smith discovered that evening that Phelps' mother worked in the other tower which was unharmed. Still, it was a scary moment.

The next day Phelps had another scary moment as he was knocked to the floor from behind as he tried to complete a breakaway layup. Fortunately, he escaped with just a badly bruised elbow. The word is "escaped" because the injury could have easily been more severe.

For some reason, Phelps seemed to attract injuries.

Again he was "lucky" in the ACC Tournament semifinals with Virginia, as the injury was a badly bruised tailbone. However, he was in pain for a couple of weeks and could not play in the final against Georgia Tech.

* Watching Phelps, the nation's best defensive player, shut down Cincinnati's Nick Van Exel, who had 21 points in the first 15 minutes of the East Regional final and only two after Phelps was assigned strictly to him.

* Matt Wenstrom coming off the bench to score eight first-half points and keep Carolina in the game, making that miracle 21-point comeback against Florida State possible.

* That remarkable nine-point run in the closing moments of the final game which took Carolina from a four-point deficit to a five-point lead against Michigan. First, there was an almost casual 3-pointer by Williams after Phelps had broken a Wolverine press; then Reese hit Phelps for a layup on a fastbreak; Lynch made a turn-around jumper from the lane; and then Lynch hit Montross on yet another inbounds play for a dunk.

* Pat Sullivan calmly sinking the key free throw to give the Tar Heels their two-point lead in the final game while Michigan players were jabbering at him about the NCAA championship riding on his shot.

* Seeing the off-court development of guys like Reese and Williams, who had not been interviewed a lot in the past, but learned to handle themselves well in the face of mounting media attention as the season progressed.

People make jokes all the time about the way Smith talks about his seniors. I know he honestly feels they are the keys to his teams. He would never admit any group is more special than another, just as he would never compare any of his teams.

However, I have to believe he has special admiration for this senior class and the way they accepted their roles:

Travis Stephenson, the non-scholarship player, who was happy to be on the team and to do whatever was needed in practice.

Scott Cherry, who drew scant recruiting attention but made so much progress in his time here that he became an important spot player.

Wenstrom, who didn't play as much as he could have at some other schools because of the presence of Montross and Kevin Salvadori, but who never complained. Instead, he did everything he could to make them better players and was ready when called on as in the Florida State game.

Rodl, an early-season regular who saw Williams take his starting spot, but continued to make big plays down the stretch.

And then there was Lynch, a sensational player, but perhaps an even better leader. He was a great rebounder and defender, but also a fine passer and scorer. He was the one who told his teammates to forget cutting down the nets at the East Regional, that there was a bigger prize awaiting them in New Orleans.

Then he went out and made sure of that with his big plays at the end of the Michigan game. On a special team with a special coach, he was indeed a very special player. ∎

Rick Brewer, a 1971 Carolina graduate, is assistant athletic director for sports information and public relations.

UNC Chorus: 'How 'Bout Them Heels!'

BY WOODY DURHAM

I knew this national championship had set Tar Heel hearts afire across the country. But I'm not sure I realized to what degree Carolina fans were embracing this team and season until two days after the national championship win over Michigan.

I was at Augusta National Golf Club to watch the practice round the Wednesday of Masters week. I was amazed at how many Carolina fans were there and how many light blue shirts, caps, buttons and other Tar Heel paraphernalia I saw. Total strangers would pass each other, notice the other's Carolina garb and say, "How 'bout them Heels!"

I noticed in the par-three tournament Davis Love III was wearing Carolina blue slacks and a stick-on logo of a Tar Heel on his cap. Jim Nantz of CBS-TV spoke to him and they talked for a minute about the game. I remember having such a warm feeling of satisfaction walking around this famous golf course, more than 300 miles from Chapel Hill, and seeing all this "Carolina connection" at the Masters.

It seems like only yesterday my wife Jean and I were on an airplane crossing the Pacific to Hawaii for the Rainbow Classic. I told Jean then, "I think Carolina's a pretty good basketball team. We'll know for sure on our way back." After losing by one point to Michigan in Honolulu, I was sold. I *knew* the Tar Heels were good. I thought Michigan was the best team in the country in late December

and Chris Webber was the best player. Seeing Webber for the first time out there, I was convinced television doesn't do him justice. You've got to see him in person to appreciate his ability.

Fourteen weeks later, we were back playing Michigan again—this time for the national championship. Webber was just as good as before, if not better. I remember several times during the game thinking that if Carolina lost, it would be because of Chris Webber. If Michigan was going to win, Webber would win it for them.

In the end, that was partially Michigan's undoing. The Wolverines clearly didn't have the team cohesiveness that the Tar Heels always have and, this year, had more of than I can remember in a long time.

Coach Steve Fisher was asked before the game about any advantages Michigan might have by being in the championship game again. He said he thought the stress of the 1992 title game showed in the last eight minutes against Duke, that the players fragmented and tried to do too much individually. Fisher said that lesson helped the Wolverines earlier this season, but I felt they made some of those same mistakes in this final. At the end, there was a lot of individuality instead of team stuff.

That's why Webber got caught bringing the ball upcourt before calling that timeout. Few people have noticed that Derrick Phelps did a great job denying Jalen Rose the ball when Webber looked to him before taking the ball upcourt himself. But if I'm Jalen Rose in that situation, I do whatever I have to do to get open to get the basketball. I'm the point guard, the national championship is on the line, and it's my job to bring the ball upcourt and direct the offense.

There's an interesting sidelight to the no-call on Webber's obvious travel in front of the Carolina bench. Hank Nichols, the NCAA supervisor of officials, later asked official Jim Stupin, who was right on the play, how he missed or why he didn't call the travel. Webber had actually been trying to call a timeout after getting the rebound of Pat Sullivan's missed free throw. In that setting, with the national title on the line, Stupin told Nichols he wanted to "help the kid" and not call a technical on him in that situation. Stupin looked away from Webber, hoping the player would figure out the situation and realize he didn't have a timeout to call. In that instant of looking away, Stupin just didn't see Webber's foot slide.

Webber might not have realized Michigan was out of timeouts, but everyone listening on the Tar Heel Sports Network was very much aware of it. Jimmy Jackson called Michigan's last timeout with 46 seconds left and Carolina up, 72-69. We said right then it was Michigan's third and final timeout. Then, coming out of the break as play resumed, Mick Mixon said it again. Carolina turned the ball over, and Webber scored to cut it to 72-71. Then Mick said, again, Michigan was out of timeouts because they couldn't stop the clock with the made basket.

So we knew immediately the consequences when Webber called the timeout after Phelps and George Lynch ran him into a deep trap in the corner. That was a technical the officials could not avoid calling because Webber was clearly signaling for the "T."

I was careful at that point not to say anything about the Tar Heels winning the national championship. I was confident by then of a victory—with Donald Williams going to the foul line for two shots and Carolina getting the ball—but I didn't want to say so yet.

In 1982, when James Worthy got the throwaway pass from Fred Brown, I said, "How 'bout them Heels! The Tar Heels are going to win the national championship!" Then I saw Coach Smith settling everyone down, still coaching, and I thought, "Whoa. This thing's not over." Worthy then missed both foul shots and Sleepy Floyd was just short on a heave from midcourt. What if that ball had gone in after what I'd said? I would have gone to my grave thinking I'd jinxed them out of it. So this year, I was careful not to refer to it until Donald made the first of his second set of two foul shots. That gave Carolina a 76-71 lead with eight seconds left and made it a two-possession game.

Finally, I was comfortable enough to say, "The Tar Heels are going to win the national championship!"

I remember the feeling in 1982 as being one of such relief, that Dean Smith finally had his national championship. This year I just kind of felt like, "Well, it's time for celebration." I think Carolina people are so happy for the team and for Coach Smith because now, no matter what happens from here, the second national title is

HUGH MORTON

kind of the icing on the cake for him.

I think, in closing, that it's very important right now for all Carolina fans to stop and think carefully about what we're watching here. Phil Ford made the point at several Educational Foundation meetings last spring that he doesn't think people appreciate that they're a part of something very special in athletics history.

I sincerely believe we might be watching something that will never be equaled in college basketball.

Dean Smith is 101 wins behind Adolph Rupp's all-time victory record. At 62, he has a few more years to surpass Rupp's record, and he appears nowhere close to thinking about retirement. He's said before that having the record doesn't interest him, that he'd retire one

Chris Webber's presence was so imposing that not even the defense of Tar Heel George Lynch could stop him.

HUGH MORTON

Dean Smith and
assistants (L-R) Phil
Ford, Randy Wiel and
Bill Guthridge plot
strategy during Final
Four practice session.

victory shy of the mark if it came to that.

But I'm starting to notice a groundswell of support that, I think, could influence Coach Smith into feeling more comfortable about passing Rupp.

Chancellor Paul Hardin told Coach Smith on the golf course shortly after the Final Four, "Dean, I think you should get the record for the University. I know you're not interested in it for yourself. But wouldn't it be wonderful for the University?"

And I think every player, manager and assistant coach over the years would love to feel like, if Dean Smith became the No. 1 coach of all-time, a little part of that record belonged to them. He was uncomfortable with the new arena bearing his name, but he said he'd accept it since they couldn't put the names of all his players on the building. In the same vein, I think if all his players asked him to go for the record—*for them*—I think he might look at it differently.

Once he had the record, I don't think it would ever be touched. Times have changed so much the last 10 years. There's so much money for coaches today, just as there is for athletes, there's not the incentive to coach or play as long. You look at some of the baseball records, the Hank Aaron and Babe Ruth records, those will never be broken because with all the money these guys get paid, none will want to play long enough to break them.

What Dean Smith has done at Carolina is so amazing that it's almost beyond description. And you look at the players returning and the players coming in, this might be one of the best stretches of his distinguished career coming up.

It's something we all should watch, enjoy and appreciate for the next few years. Like Phil Ford says, we're a part of something special and we may never see it again. ■

Woody Durham (UNC 1963) has been the "Voice of the Tar Heels" since 1971.

FROM BOURBON STREET ...

...TO FRANKLIN STREET

Tar Heel fans celebrate in New Orleans and Chapel Hill following NCAA title win over Michigan April 5.

N'Awlins Weekend Scrapbook For Life.

B Y L E E P A C E

The pink slips with phone messages were scattered all over John Cherry's desk that early April afternoon amid a half-eaten sandwich, a Superdome seating chart and computerized printouts of Educational Foundation point standings. The voice on the speaker phone droned on and on. The caller sounded desperate.

"John, I've *got* to get there," the man said, halfway pleading. "How does it look?"

Cherry looked at the numbers on his computer screen and shook his head. "Not very good," he answered.

The job Cherry and other staff members at the Educational Foundation had leading to the Final Four was a difficult one. They had less than 3,000 tickets to distribute and many thousands of Carolina fans who wanted them. And a hotel room. And an airplane seat.

Demand was so high that the Foundation limited ticket applicants to those with 400 or more points accumulated over time through contributions. That represents roughly the upper seven percent of the Foundation's 11,000 members.

The plan was simple: Start at the top of the points list and offer members four tickets for purchase—until they run out. In 1982 and 1991, Carolina's last two Final Four appearances, every member who wanted tickets was accommo-dated. But this was out of sight. "It's the only fair way we know to do it," Cherry said. "It's a combination of the Final Four being in New Orleans and people having a good feeling that we might win it."

"John, I was there in '82. I *can't* miss it," the caller said.

"We'll know something tonight," Cherry told him. "We'll call and let you know."

The man finally hung up.

"How'd you like to do this 15 hours a day?" Cherry asked. Then he smiled.

"But it beats what Duke's doing now."

***

For those able to find their way to New Orleans for the 1993 Final Four, the experience was one for the archives. Everyone has a birth date, a wedding date, a baptism or bar mitzvah. So too should all fans see their team win the national title in the Big Easy.

Add this up: The Final Four ... your very first one ... in New Orleans ... against heavyweight programs like Kansas, Michigan and Kentucky ... with a Tar Heel team that had more personality, drive and ability than any in recent memory ... with the delicious subplots of Roy Williams and the Fab Five and the Monster Mash from bluegrass country ... with a semifinal win over a Kansas team that nailed the Heels two years ago, that sorry scene ending with Dean Smith being ejected for a misdemeanor ... the whole thing capped off by a pulsating win over the Woof-erines for the NCAA championship.

The result measures a google on the pleasure meter.

The Franklin Street party was well under way that warm March Sunday after the Tar Heels threw an arrogant fish from Cincinnati back into the Ohio River. My wife, Catherine, had a suggestion:

"Let's go to New Orleans," she said.

"No way," I answered. "Not enough money and not enough time."

"*Let's go to New Orleans,*" she growled.

"Okay," I said.

HUGH MORTON

We faced a financial decision at the outset: We could fly and do New Orleans on the cheap; or we could drive and eat well. We chose the latter, and shortly after 9 a.m. on Friday were wheeling west on Hwy. 54 around Carrboro. My calculations were for a drive of about 850 miles and 13 hours on the road. I began pushing buttons on the radio control, found WCHL, and the strains from that old song came eerily through the speaker:

"Here we come, New Orleans.

"The Tar Heels love New Orleans.

"We're going to Lou-siana,

"To bring home Number One."

It was the song by the Fabulous Flyers introduced in 1982 and played all week prior to Carolina's first New Orleans Final Four. The Shrunken Head, a Franklin Street souvenir and T-shirt shop, had some 45s stored away and brought them back out this year.

"That could be a good omen," I said.

The Tar Heels would need lots of good omens in New Orleans, and there were plenty to go around. Catherine found a heads-up penny in the ladies bathroom at halftime of the Michigan game. One fan on Bourbon Street sported a Tar Heel logo *very* low on his abdomen, which he wasn't shy volunteering to show female passers-by. One saloon featured a custom-made libation called the "N.C. Tar Bomb"—Jack Daniels, peach brandy and light-blue food color.

The city was a beehive of activity as fans from Chapel Hill, Lexington, Lawrence and Ann Arbor descended for a four-day minimum of revelry (to get a hotel room, you had to pay for four nights, no matter who won or lost). There was also a PGA Tour event the same weekend, as well as two conventions. But New Orleans handled it all with the efficiency of a host that had entertained Sugar Bowl, St. Patrick's Day and Mardi Gras throngs already this year.

"This town loves a party," said one local, noting there were seven bars for every one church.

On this N'Awlins weekend, there was never enough time. There was another pep rally to attend, another T-shirt to buy, another tune from the Neville Brothers or Harry Connick Jr. to enjoy, another old classmate to run into, another aspirin to pop, another piece of New Orleans history to delve into—from the tomb of Marie Laveau, the voodoo queen buried in St. Louis Cemetery, to the house on St. Peter Street where Tennessee Williams wrote *A Streetcar Named Desire.*

And, good gracious, there was always another fork to fill: with beignets at Cafe du Monde; with poached eggs and hollandaise for breakfast or bananas Foster for dessert at Brennan's; with Creole bouillabaisse at Galatoire's; with etouffée and gumbo and jambalaya from any of dozens of cozy haunts in the French Quarter. (For my tastes, though,

they can *keep* the chicory.) Perhaps tastiest of all: a munchie-busting, foot-long hotdog from a street vendor at 2:30 a.m. after your team's won the national title, piping hot with chili, onions, Dijon mustard, Tabasco and Creole seasoning.

A few snapshots from the French Quarter:

* The pair of women's legs protruding from the window of a dolly bar and the psychedelic signs beckoning guests to enter and watch the female mud-wrestling and assorted other burlesque entertainment inside.

* The mimes and the statuesque poses they held seemingly forever; the tap-dancers with their rapid-fire footwork; and the rattle of pocket change in the cigar boxes each entertainer brought to collect a day's wages.

* The sidewalk band cranking out a Bob Dylan number, the lead singer wailing, "How does it *feeeeeeell?*" the drummer cracking his sticks on the cement and a drunk across the street banging out time on an empty newspaper rack.

* The Elton John-lookalike at Lucky Pierre's, a Bourbon Street saloon accented with hot pink walls and framed photos of lingerie-clad women in honor of the building's heritage as a brothel; he wore oversized glasses and a balloon hat and could knock out everything from *Crocodile Rock* to *Levon* on the piano.

* The young rap dancers down at Jackson Square beside the Mississippi River who could do feats far more impressive than anything I've seen from Michael Jordan. (Just how *do* they spin like a top on their shoulders on hard cement?)

* The smiles on everyone's face in Pat O'Brien's courtyard Saturday afternoon, where the blue-clad fans of Carolina, Michigan, Kentucky and Kansas were sipping Hurricanes. The band played each school's fight song and, for this moment anyway, anything was possible.

* And, of course, the snap, crackle and pop of Bourbon Street late Monday night, the national title safely in tow.

SCOTT SHARPE/THE NEWS & OBSERVER

Tickets were tough to come by for Tar Heel fans, but just being there was half the fun.

The Tar Heel players were there, along about midnight, after a rousing welcome at the Hotel Inter-Continental and a quick change of clothes. Former Tar Heels like Jimmy Black and Matt Doherty, both members of the 1982 Tar Heels now in the college coaching ranks, were there. So was King Rice, today an assistant coach at Oregon.

Former Duke player Brian Davis was there, catching an occasional barb from Heel fans, and finally the Michigan team and Chris Webber braved the denizens in search of solace from a disheartening loss. Amidst the intoxication of victory and barley, some fans forgot Webber is only 20 years old and a human being and peppered him with shouts of, "Hey, Chris, get a 'T'!" To his credit, the Michigan manchild punched no one in the snout.

More deserving of some razzing was ESPN commentator Dick Vitale, who was effervescent earlier in the evening with his pick of Michigan by five. As soon as Vitale was spotted walking down Bourbon Street, Tar Heel fans smothered his path.

"Time out, BAY-BEE!!!" the crescendo went. "Michigan by FIVE! Way to go, Vitale, BAY-BEE!!!"

Everywhere Black and Doherty went, the feelings were just like 11 years ago, when they joined starters Jordan, Sam Perkins and James Worthy in hoisting the gorilla off Dean Smith's back.

"It was just like our team won again," Black said. "It was just like reliving 1982 all over."

Doherty, now an assistant to Roy Williams at Kansas, has had little occasion the last three years to get to know Derrick Phelps, but in the din of Bourbon Street both recognized and respected each other's contributions to Tar Heel basketball and hugged each other affectionately.

"There's a common thread there that bonds us all together," Doherty says. "It doesn't matter when you played. It's all one brotherhood."

***

The Old Absinthe Bar at the corner of Bourbon and Iberville Streets in New Orleans has been in business since 1806. In its early days, a sailor would often take a dollar bill, write his name on it and pin it to the wall of the bar, so upon his return to New Orleans from sea, he'd have at least $1 to his name. The custom caught on with tourists, and today an estimated $30,000 worth of cash is stapled to the walls.

At 2:10 the morning of Tuesday, April 6, I took a stool beside the bar, ordered a beer and took two $1 bills and a pen from my pocket. I carefully inscribed one bill, then the next, and handed them to the bartender to attach to the wall.

I went back into the night, my message remaining on the Old Absinthe's walls, hopefully to hang there another 187 years:

UNC 77, Michigan 71. ■

Freelance writer Lee Pace (Carolina 1979) writes often about Tar Heel basketball and football.

HUGH MORTON

Black, Jordan, Doherty during quiet moment in 1982; Black and Doherty returned in '93.

Victory Party Some Enchanted Evening.

BY DAVE GLENN

On a cold and rainy April evening in a place they call the Southern Part of Heaven, at just about midnight, the words came over the police radio dispatcher as clear as day:

"There's a burning couch moving down Franklin Street ... repeat ... there's a burning couch moving down Franklin Street."

Carolina 77, Michigan 71.

That's how it all began.

During a postgame interview, amidst a crazy, raucous Superdome setting in New Orleans, UNC center Eric Montross wondered aloud what it would be like to be back on campus.

"I wish there was some way they could just beam us up to Chapel Hill, where we could enjoy this with our friends and our fans," Montross said. "I'm sure things are getting pretty wild up there right now."

No kidding.

Just minutes before, with a mere 30 seconds remaining in the championship game, the streets of Chapel Hill were virtually motionless. Dozens of police officers stood guard on Franklin Street in anticipation of the coming events, and occasional screams and moans echoed from local bars and residences, but all in all it could've passed for just another night on The Hill.

The bars were stuffed to the gills with Carolina fans, some of whom had come from as far away as Florida, California and Canada just to enjoy this special Monday night on their old stomping grounds. Beverages flowed freely on "Bourbon Street North," inside and outside, as the rule of law took a back seat to a more important agenda. On this night of nights, this most famous college town—once noted for having the highest per capita beer consumption in the nation—did nothing to damage its reputation.

"Our tab?" said one older gentleman quizzically, when asked how much his group had spent in Spanky's, a restaurant-bar on East Franklin Street. "Oh my God, OUR TAB!!"

Many of those same fans had arrived before noon—armed with school work, newspapers, even a computer in one case—just to get good seats at their favorite bars for the 9:22 p.m. tipoff. "They were waiting at our door when we opened up this morning," said a worker at Ham's, a restaurant-bar on West Franklin Street. "I mean, 12 hours early to watch a basketball game! It was unbelievable. I've never seen anything like it."

A few hundred yards away, on the UNC campus, a powerful buzzing sound roared out of Carmichael Auditorium. More than 7,000 fans gathered in the Tar Heels' old home to watch the much-anticipated title matchup on a 300-square-foot television screen, where Godzilla-sized versions of Montross and his talented teammates would soon become larger than life in more ways than one.

By the time the final buzzer sounded, and Dean Smith and the boys in blue were cutting down the nets in the Crescent City, downtown Chapel Hill exploded into a colorful array of vivid artistry, splendiferous fireworks and sparkling smiles.

The Carmichael throng made a beeline for Franklin Street. Hundreds of fraternity and sorority members raced from their nearby houses to join the fray. Thousands of bar patrons sprinted over, around and through tables, chairs and their fellow fans in a frenzied attempt to join the growing masses on the barricaded street outside.

The celebration had undoubtedly begun.

One individual slowly walked up to the glass door of a Franklin Street bank and meticulously finger-painted a "#1" logo that managed to stay around long enough to welcome the bank's employees early Tuesday morning. Others aimlessly threw paint—"It's okay, it's water-based," one man yelled to an approaching police officer—on cars, storefronts and everyone and anything that fell in their paths. Another man, completely oblivious to his collapsing surroundings, calmly walked down the middle of the street with a paint roller, leaving a foot-wide stripe of Carolina blue in his wake.

"You've heard of painting the town red?" said the man, smiling the most genuine of smiles. "Well, I'm going to paint this town blue if it takes me all night."

"We did it!" yelled a woman in a gray Carolina sweatshirt, running and jumping with hands raised for all the world to see before disappearing into the burgeoning crowd.

Within minutes, the mass of people on Franklin Street had doubled, tripled and quadrupled in size. People of all ages, all colors and all backgrounds converged aimlessly from every direction. High-fives, chants and hugs abounded. At the evening's peak, about 30 minutes after the end of the game, a crowd of more than 20,000 had taken to the streets of Chapel Hill.

"If there's a bigger party in this world," yelled one exhausted fan as he nudged through the crowd, "I sure as hell want to find it."

Fireworks exploded from the rooftops high above a cold, rain-soaked crowd that had grown into an elbow-to-elbow mass of humanity stretched from Rosemary Street to Columbia Street and beyond. "Look at the sky," screamed a little girl in a Carolina jumpsuit, giggling in amazement at her wondrous surroundings from her mother's arms. Hundreds of onlookers appeared on Franklin Street rooftops, braving the near-freezing temperatures, screaming at strangers and surveying the furor below.

Several barechested young men bumped their way through the crowd, full-sized couch in hand, seeking to add fuel to the piddling bonfire in the middle of Franklin Street. The ensuing ashes and rising flames brought the crowd's roar to an exciting crescendo for all the world to see. Roll after roll of toilet paper flew toward the sky, bounding from limb to limb to hang amongst the trees or falling into the puddles on the ground to form a white, pasty mush. Several young men climbed lightposts on either side of the street for a better perspective.

Three more college-aged kids raced to the corner of Franklin and Columbia Streets, where the local news crews had gathered for an up-close-and-personal look at what had become an evening of pure, unadulterated bliss. The rowdy, fist-pumping trio had prepared a special message for a certain television announcer, a note they scrawled on an old bedsheet and unfurled for Monday's late-night news: "Dick Vitale, you missed the pick tonight, *baby*!!"

The Monday night madness was carefully and unobtrusivefully chaperoned by more than 100 police officers, some of them from the Durham County Sheriff's Department, the State Highway Patrol or as far away as the Burlington Police Department. An overwhelming majority of the officers, many of them grinning Tar Heel fans, seemed to enjoy their small participation in the home team's success.

"We had a little trial run for this kind of thing when the Grateful Dead were in town for a concert last week," said one officer, whose department-issued shoes took on an interesting blue hue at some point early in the celebration. "But this is a whole lot more fun."

One stumbling coed approached one of the out-of-town policemen, rolled her eyes at the

BOB DONNAN

Those who survived the suds and slop, the chill and thrill of Franklin Street could memorialize their night with a T-shirt made for the occasion.

I WAS THERE!
FRANKLIN STREET 1993
CAROLINA   MICHIGAN
77   71

BOB DONNAN

prominent Durham logo on his chest and arms and slurred a most pungent question about his underlying loyalties.

"You weren't pulling for *them*, were you?"

"No, ma'am," the officer replied with a smile, "I'm a Tar Heel born and bred. You mean there's a basketball team in Durham?"

Heaven, indeed.

Of course, as the night grew colder, the fans grew bolder.

Unbridled in their joy that the Tar Heels had pulled it off, the Carolina faithful decided to do the same, stripping off shirts, shoes and—yes, even pants and other "unnecessary" articles of clothing—as Franklin Street developed into a scene something like a 20,000-strong locker-room celebration. A group of approximately 20 males offered its own special contribution to this most enchanted evening by sprinting down the sidewalk wearing about as much clothing as Montross has hair on his head.

In the end, most who were there would agree on one thing: Few dreams and fairy tales could approach the magical night of Monday, April 5, 1993, in Chapel Hill, North Carolina.

Children danced, strangers embraced and grown men cried in a town-wide emotional celebration of almost unparalleled proportions.

Tensions eased, problems disappeared. For a few brief moments, all was right in the world.

By 3 a.m., most of the crowd had wandered home to reality. By morning, town public works employees had Franklin Street (except for a few uprooted trees) glistening once again, as if the entire evening had been one, big, crazy dream.

Time continued to run, of course, the world continued to spin—more for some than others—and the cold, harsh realities of work, exams and life lay ahead.

Only the diehards remained on this late night, kicking through the bonfire ashes, sloshing through puddles on the pasty white street, telling their stories to the darkness around them.

Finally, the Southern Part of Heaven fell silent once again. The streets, finally empty. The memories, ever full.

"This is one of the greatest days of my entire life," shouted a seemingly sober man in his mid-40s, little boy in tow, as they wandered away into the empty night. "I'll never forget this as long as I live." ∎

Dave Glenn (UNC 1990) has written for "Carolina Court" and is a third-year UNC law student.

Score looms overhead as George Lynch addresses Smith Center welcoming party Tuesday afternoon.

The Circle Is Closed For Carolina Family.

BY ALFRED HAMILTON JR.

The telephone in our Chicago home rang every 10 minutes until 3 in the morning on April 6. And when it wasn't ringing, we were calling North Carolina. Our 21-year-old son at Chapel Hill called about six times, happier with each call, and with each Bud Light. The old friends calling shared in some sense of relief, that a cake had been baked, a circle closed. My last thought of Carolina and Dean Smith before falling asleep was, "Finally, we don't have to defend him from *any* of the bastards."

***

Thirty-six years ago in March, Dean Smith was in Kansas City interviewing for an assistant coach's job at North Carolina. The Tar Heels were in KC on their way to a six-overtime weekend, a national title and a 32-0 record.

My parents had allowed their 13-year-old to fly to Kansas City against all conventional wisdom. No more than 100 Carolina followers actually went out there, and nobody called it the "Final Four." But my mother somehow understood its importance, and life since has never been quite the same for me.

Back then, basketball players had more time for little boys. Among the 1957 Tar Heels, reserve guard Ken Rosemond had time for me. He carried me off the court on his back after Joe Quigg hit those totally improbable free throws against Kansas. We walked together in the rain back to Carolina's hotel, Rosemond still in uniform because Municipal Auditorium had no lockerrooms.

I saw Rosemond off and on for the next three decades or so, most often at basketball games. He coached for years, a few with Dean Smith, and later built a clothing business in Durham. In my Carolina undergraduate years in the early '60s, my future wife often spent the weekend nights with the Rosemonds just outside Chapel Hill.

Ken Rosemond died of cancer only days after Carolina's title triumph over Michigan, becoming the first departed among the 1957 Tar Heel players. He was the oldest of those once-young men, and his death begins to close the circle. He scored only 17 points in that shining season 36 years ago, but he was a star nonetheless.

Rosemond, like many others, found his life intertwined with Carolina basketball. This mingling with people's lives is inevitable for Coach Smith, given a 32-year stretch of excellence at a university so many people care about.

I suppose around 50,000 people have graduated from Chapel Hill since the university took a chance on the young Frank McGuire assistant. Consider how many of those lives have been touched by the drama of UNC basketball. Imagine how many times Carolina alumni have gathered around television sets, all over the country, just to feel like part of it all.

For Smith and Bill Guthridge, though, the players and managers best represent the passage of time, the turning of circles. Almost 200 players and student managers have won varsity letters under Smith. As long as they want to be, they will belong to the Carolina basketball family.

The circles keep closing in the family. Hugh Donohue, Larry Brown, Billy Cunningham, Charlie Shaffer and Richard Vinroot have seen their children enroll at Carolina. I didn't get a count, but Coach Smith must have 75 varsity "grandchildren" by now.

For those of us who were in school when the Smith era began, there is also a sense of "belonging" to basketball at Carolina. Each of us has a set of memories. It is among the things defining our adulthoods, something we pass on to children.

Almost 25 years to the day after my walk in the rain in Kansas City, I stood with my 10-year-old son on a windy and wet day outside the Louisiana Superdome, absolutely terrified that Georgetown would defeat Carolina in the 1982 title game. We called my mother in Raleigh for some assurance.

A few hours later, we watched on the Iberville Street sidewalk as the Tar Heels came back to the French Quarter with the NCAA title plaque. My son didn't know it at the time, but his life has never been the same since.

Only 11 years ago it was, but so many things in the Carolina family have kept working toward the full circle. Jordan's ascendancy, Worthy at the end of his warrior years, Sweet D retired, the friendly assistant coach who is now a near-legend at Kansas, even deaths in the family. Not much is unchanged, except perhaps men named Smith and Guthridge.

A few years ago, that 10-year-old in New Orleans had himself changed into a college freshman, and played a little junior varsity basketball at Carolina. Even though he may not have scored much more than 17 points in the whole season, he closed a circle with that uniform.

Smith's second New Orleans championship team, in hindsight, brought together so many fundamental principles that have been taught over 32 years. It was a team that could not win without selfless play, could not have won in late March and early April without attention to every detail, including keeping up with timeouts. This team forever certified basketball played the Smith way.

Unlike the 1982 champion, this one really could go nine deep, 10 in a pinch. But this team did not have two certain Hall of Fame members, nor did it carry national championship credentials for much of the season. Like all great Smith teams, however, it to was be burdened with that incessant pressure to win at the end.

And bless their hearts, they didn't shoot that well at times, and the flaw might have been fatal. But not after Donald "The Assassin" Williams uncovered his guns. The final 3-pointer that simply executed Cincinnati in the East Regional, that three-quarter twist rocket, must have thoroughly pleased Lennie Rosenbluth.

***

On Thursday of Final Four week, the day before the Tar Heels flew to New Orleans, it was supposed to rain in Chapel Hill. Instead it was windy and sun-splashed, the tired gray trees in the Old Chapel Hill Cemetery trying to bloom once again.

It was time for my father's funeral. He had struggled in recent years and there was more reflection than grief as we looked at my mother's 1990 headstone, and my father's new grave alongside. The universal circle had closed for me and my brothers. I don't remember anyone saying anything about basketball, but we probably did. Given the chance, my mother surely would have.

Maybe mentioning basketball at a parent's funeral is incongruous, but not so much for us who were in Chapel Hill when Coach Smith started his glorious trip that will be forever known as the Smith years. Carolina basketball has been mentioned at plenty of funerals by now.

Besides that, the old cemetery is a good place to think about Carolina basketball. You're surrounded by fine Chapel Hill natives, after all, mostly people of achievement, and many of them fond of Carolina athletics once upon a time.

Best of all, you can actually see a lot of Carolina basketball history from these old graves. The Tin Can site was up the street, where we were playing intramurals when Coach Smith took over. Woollen Gym is nearby, where Frank McGuire's office doubled as a ticket booth and Coach Smith was hanged in effigy. Carmichael is next door, carrying its indelible memories of three consecutive Final Four teams, Jordan, Ford Corners, Miller, Davis and Worthy.

Remember, too, that national basketball titles were brought home to each of these places. Kenny Rosemond came home from Kansas City right down there on Woollen's front steps.

And look due south through the early-blooming trees around the end of the basketball season, and you can see the top of the Smith Center. Now, it too is home for a national championship team.

For all of us who started with Coach Smith, there isn't much left to do except be grateful. We have precious little room for more pride and joy. We have grown up with a coach and players who have never let anyone down. Go ahead and win, you Tar Heels of 1993-94 and beyond. But it won't be easy to make some of us any happier than we are today.

Our circle is closed. ■

Alfred T. Hamilton Jr. is a 1965 Carolina graduate and former managing editor of "The Greensboro Record." His work has appeared in "March to the Top" and "Carolina Court." Hamilton lives in Chicago, where is is marketing director for Recycled Paper Products Inc.

After 25 Years, It's Time To Celebrate.

BY LARRY KEITH

So, anyway, there I was on the night of April 5th eating dinner with Kareem Abdul-Jabbar in New Orleans and replaying the 1968 UCLA-North Carolina mismatch when someone told me I had a phone call from the *Sports Illustrated* managing editor.

None of the above happens every day, I can assure you, so let me enjoy my reverie.

When I went to the phone, Mark (I'm sorry, Mark Mulvoy) said that if North Carolina beat Michigan in the game to be played in a few hours, he wanted me to write a story for an *SI* commemorative issue on the Tar Heels' championship season. I gave my assent.

My journalistic objectivity concerning Carolina basketball has been tested many times over the years. Like most people who grew up in North Carolina and attended school in Chapel Hill, I bleed Carolina blue, too. But when I was covering the team as sports editor of *The Daily Tar Heel* (1967-68), sports director of WCHL radio (1968-69) and, finally, as *Sports Illustrated's* college basketball writer (1976-80) and editor (1980-84), I wrapped myself in the White Phantom robe of professionalism. This is the pristine cloak I wore in 1980 when I boldly omitted my alma mater from the *SI* preseason Top 20, only to watch it reach the championship game. Talk about mixed emotions.

On this fine New Orleans evening, however, there was delicious irony, a feeling of life coming full circle. Twenty-five years before I had watched Jabbar, then known as Lew Alcindor, absolutely devour the Tar Heels in the championship game at the Los Angeles Sports Arena. Now I was watching Jabbar devour dinner in a private club overlooking the Superdome. As an undergraduate, I had written that UNC travelled 3,000 miles to lose by 7 feet, 1 inch. Now, as *Sports Illustrated's* editorial projects director, I was telling him how Rusty Clark, his opposing center in that game, had become a surgeon. Kareem remarked good humoredly that he wouldn't have thought Rusty had the hands for that line of work.

"Who do you like in the game tonight?" I asked.

"North Carolina," he said.

The man sure knows his basketball, though.

I agreed with him, of course, but then, I have always liked the Tar Heels in the championship game. I liked them in 1977 against Marquette, but in the final seconds my reporter's instincts had me kneeling beside Warrior Coach Al McGuire to get a close look at his tears of joy, while my own tears were for Dean Smith.

Four years later, as a senior editor chastened by my Top 20 *faux pas* in the preseason, I liked Carolina against Indiana, but I dispassionately edited the story about the Hoosiers' victory. The next year in New Orleans, I rooted from the stands as the Tar Heels beat Houston on Saturday and returned to the office for the magazine's Tuesday morning close of the championship game on Monday night. This time Carolina won, but Curry Kirkpatrick's story was coming in, and I had a job to do. The celebrating would come later (much later, it turned out.)

Later was 1993. I attended the two regional games across the Hudson River in New Jersey with my 13- and 15-year-old sons, sitting beside former Carolina assistant coach John Lotz and just a few seats away from Dr. Linnea Smith. Welcome to Tar Heel Country. My younger son, Teddy Tar Heel, was keeping a scrapbook of Tar Heel clippings (something I might have done at his age) as well as a video record gleaned from ESPN *SportsCenter* reports (something I never could have imagined anyone doing.)

Then it was off to New Orleans, with my wife Carolyn. It was clear that I could not pull this off myself, that I needed all the family support I could muster. My choices were somewhat limited, however. Back at my ecumenical home in Garden City, our 10-year-old daughter, Christine, was sleeping in her 1992 Duke championship T-shirt, and our six-year-old son, Andrew, was wearing his Clemson hat and rooting hard for anybody North Carolina played. This sort of deviant behavior can be expected when one brother-in-law attended Duke and another Clemson.

It was fun being a fan. In the semifinal win over Kansas, I talked to former Las Vegas Coach Jerry Tarkanian, who declared that Donald Williams was the best shooter in the country. I thought the Shark might be exaggerating a bit, but later events proved he might be correct. On Monday afternoon before the championship game, I attended a Tar Heel pep rally with a *Sports Illustrated* colleague (and former Carolina pitcher) Dave Kirk. We talked to some alums and spotted another refugee from the '68 UCLA debacle, Bill Bunting. Fully recovered.

I cannot tell you anything about the final game you don't already know (and Teddy Tar Heel hasn't looked at 1,000 times on his tape of the game.) I can assure you that, true to his word, Roy Williams, the Mississippi-spittin' Kansas coach who was Dean's assistant in '82 (unlike me, he got to stay around for the final game that year), rooted like heck for Carolina. He was sitting a few rows above us, with a better sight line. The gambler in front of me, meanwhile, went crazy when he saw a late-game lineup that resembled Carolina's old Blue Team.

Minutes after Chris Webber's K.O. T.O., the concession stand near us miraculously produced some North Carolina National Champions T-shirts. Dave, my wife and I bought the last three and paraded to the Tar Heel cheering section, where we were the XL envy of all. From there we strolled to the team hotel, drank beer, stood on lobby furniture and hung with the mob until Eric Montross came back with his video camera recording the scene. (Look for me, Eric, I'm the middle-aged alum celebrating his first Tar Heel title. Everyone else, I think, had been there 11 years before.)

Back in New York, I had two days to research and write a story for the *SI* commemorative issue on the early years of Carolina basketball, from the first Bynum Hall team in 1911 to the dawn of the Frank McGuire Woollen Gym era in 1952. Because of my life passage from writing to editing in 1980, I hadn't produced an *SI* article in years. But this one was fairly easy: Cartwright Carmichael, Jack Cobb and George Glamack were as important in their day as anyone the Tar Heels have had since. Anyone.

The next week I flew to Chapel Hill with *Sports Illustrated* publisher Don Elliman for the official presentation of the commemorative issue to Coach Smith. Dean's assistant, Bill Guthridge, gave us a tour of the Dean Dome

This commemorative issue was the magazine's third following similar treatises on Alabama football and the Dallas Cowboys.

(no, Dean, he didn't call it that) and pointed out where the new banners would go. I spent the afternoon eating lunch at the Rat and checking on *SI* issue sales in old haunts like Sutton's and Jeff's. That night I had dinner (at the Rat, so think of me as the alum with the soul for nostalgia and the stomach for Tums) with *The Daily Tar Heel's* Warren Hynes. This fine young journalist had the pleasure of writing about a North Carolina national championship while he was still an undergraduate.

I, on the other, had to wait a quarter of a century. ∎

Larry Keith, a 1969 Carolina graduate, is Editorial Projects Director of "Sports Illustrated" and a member of the Board of Directors of the UNC Alumni Association. He lives in Garden City, N.Y.

Old Tar Heels Keep The Flame-Forever.

BY MARK WHICKER

It was a Sunday morning, March of 1992, and the sun hit Mitch Kupchak's smile and blinded me as we happened to walk together into the Great Western Forum.

"We're winning," Kupchak proclaimed.

"We" were not the Lakers, of whom Kupchak is assistant general manager. "We" were the Tar Heels, for whom Kupchak played center in the mid-1970s. He got to Chapel Hill just as I left. He never did leave, not really. None of them do.

I knew Kupchak was referring to North Carolina's tenuous first-half lead over Duke, the defending and upcoming NCAA champions. Kupchak was at The Forum to watch his Lakers lose to the Detroit Pistons. That was business. Events in Durham were religion.

"Yeah," I replied, "but Hurley will win it for them. They haven't lost a game this year with Hurley healthy."

Kupchak's eyes became hard marbles, as they once did in the center-jump circle in Carmichael Auditorium.

"What do you mean? We beat them when Hurley was playing."

"Yeah, but Hurley broke his foot in that game."

Kupchak grinned, as he would grin at a child who had declared two plus two equaled six.

"He didn't get hurt until the last two minutes of the game— you're into Duke now, like all the media," Kupchak said, dismissing me for the day. By then Bobby Hurley was indeed beating Carolina, but I would choose not to dredge it up.

Late this March a few days before Carolina would visit New Orleans and show how remarkably well it had survived two years of Dukedom, I phoned Franklin "Rusty" Clark.

Clark was the first, second and third of Dean Smith's Final Four centers, 1967 through 1969. Smith has called Clark his most important recruit. Clark never played in the NBA, but he still has the UNC record for rebounds in a game (30). Stupidly, I thought 24 years would remove the spiritual adhesive.

"Well, you know, a lot of people criticize Coach Smith's NCAA Tournament record— they say he's only won one title, with all the great players," I recited dutifully.

Clark's serrated reply landed hard, fiberoptically, on the ear.

"The people that write that," he snapped, "don't know anything about college basketball. They've been covering too much baseball and hockey."

So there is no shortage of bodies that will fall on the grenade that lands near Dean Smith.

In 1965, before Smith was even a certified winner, Billy Cunningham charged off a bus to keep Dean's mummified likeness from going up in flames.

That's back when you could smoke on campus.

Everybody did, back in *The Daily Tar Heel* office of the early '70s, and even in charco-broiled Carmichael, when a future Big 10 commissioner (Jim Delany) and South Carolina coach (Eddie Fogler) could be seen in the same backcourt (but, fortunately, not too often).

One day Maryland was practicing, and I introduced myself to the edgy Lefty Driesell.

"You a Daily Tar Heel?" Lefty repeated. "Boy, do I feel sorry for you. These players, they only have to be Tar Heels a couple of times a week. But you—you gotta be a Tar Heel every day!"

Even then, the Heels were feared, loathed, envied and scrutinized. And they drew their own line in the tar.

The 1971 club was the unexpected regular-season ACC champ. It savored the huzzahs it would receive in its last home game. But Don McCauley, merely the best Carolina football player between Charlie Justice and Lawrence Taylor, would also be honored.

My *Daily Tar Heel* sports page billed it as "McCauley Night."

That was not the day to get the accumulated reflections of UNC seniors Lee Dedmon, David Chadwick, Dale Gipple, Richard Tuttle and Don Eggleston. One by one, hissing from the

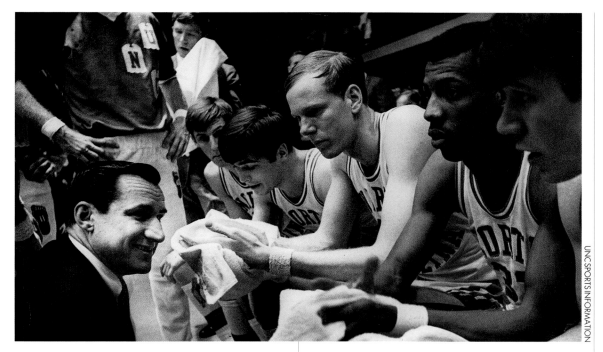

Rusty Clark, now a Fayetteville surgeon, listens intently during late-1960s huddle.

other side of the line, they said I had seriously misjudged the occasion. All but Dedmon: "I got nothing to say to you." Don McCauley be damned. Their universe was very small and very blue.

How long ago that seems. How long ago that *was*. Smith and I shared nothing but a knee-walking urge to smoke the nearest available cigarette, so I presented him with 200 of his favorite Kents, in a carton, when he won his 200th game. He was quite appreciative. They might have even lasted the weekend.

Now it's 774 wins, nine Final Four trips, two national titles, 13 straight trips to the NCAA regional semis, 16 regular-season ACC titles, and four starters back next year. The only thing that's changed is Dean has given up the weed.

Did you read about the end of the Mike Ditka era in Chicago? Some era. It lasted 10 years. Smith has coached 32 seasons. In the last 27, he has visited postseason tournaments. No team, college or pro, has been that good, that long. Why, there have only been 27 Super Bowls.

That is the hook. That is what makes Mitch Kupchak glare and Rusty Clark bristle.

For them, Carolina basketball is beyond criticism in this disposable age. It is the only place where one can witness that old-time precision. It adjusts, but it does not change.

The talented young men still come because they know Smith will honor the Old Covenant.

They must attend class, they must point to the passer, they must wear ties and they must not taunt.

In return, they will play. If they play well enough, they will be encouraged to turn pro early (imagine the '83 Heels with James Worthy, the '85 Heels with Michael Jordan).

If they cannot, they will find rewarding work somewhere.

They can be as brash as George Karl or as devout as Bobby Jones. They shoot from 22 feet like Donald Williams, and like Jeff Lebo, Brad Hoffman, Charlie Scott and other unfettered Tar Heels—if they can.

And if they ever bump hard against life, their call for help will be buzzed straight into Smith, past the reporters and the alumni and the university presidents on hold.

Carolina basketball wins in 1993 as it did in 1967.

More importantly, it works in 1993 as it did in 1967.

Name anything else that does.

So if Mitch and Rusty and James and Michael want to keep the flame, do not disturb.

They've just got to be Tar Heels, every day. ■

Mark Whicker, a 1973 Carolina graduate, has written for newspapers in Chapel Hill, Winston-Salem, Dallas and Philadelphia. For the last six years, he's been a columnist for the "Orange County Register."

introducing...

COLOURS
by
ALEXANDER JULIAN

...paint the town

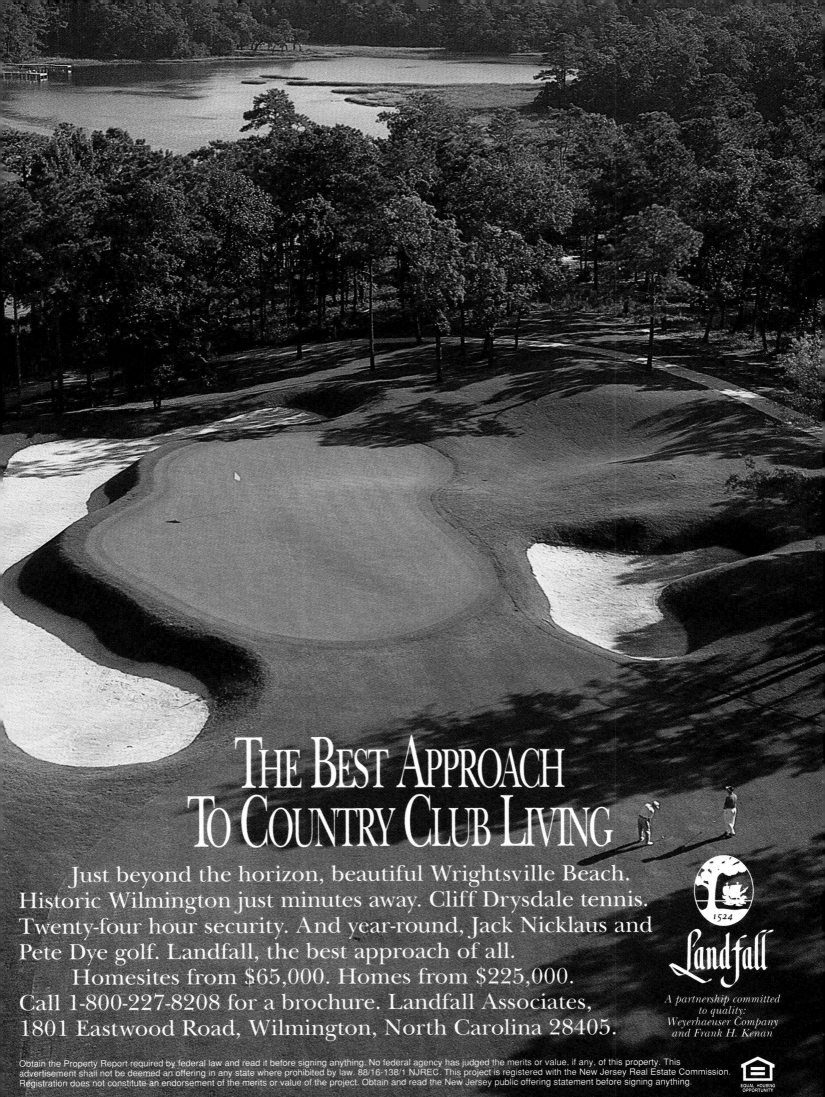

THE BEST APPROACH TO COUNTRY CLUB LIVING

Just beyond the horizon, beautiful Wrightsville Beach.
Historic Wilmington just minutes away. Cliff Drysdale tennis.
Twenty-four hour security. And year-round, Jack Nicklaus and
Pete Dye golf. Landfall, the best approach of all.
Homesites from $65,000. Homes from $225,000.
Call 1-800-227-8208 for a brochure. Landfall Associates,
1801 Eastwood Road, Wilmington, North Carolina 28405.

Landfall
1524

*A partnership committed
to quality:
Weyerhaeuser Company
and Frank H. Kenan*

We Worked Hard For Our Final Four, Too.

We join the rest of the world in congratulating the Heels on their spectacular year in basketball. For The Burris Agency and our clients, it's been an equally exciting year in advertising. At the recent 1993 Piedmont Triad Advertising Federation Addy Awards, the final count for The Burris Agency was not one, but four Best of Shows, plus ten Addys and nine Citations. We're pleased to report that our work has gone on to win District and National honors as well. Guess that's what happens when a team works hard to turn natural talent into outstanding performance.

THE BURRIS AGENCY

GREAT RELATIONSHIPS MAKE GREAT ADVERTISING.

If you'd like to see the work that swept the PTAF Addys, call Agency President and Die-Hard Tar Heel Supporter Mark Burris at 919- 884-4249.
The Burris Agency, Inc. Post Office Box 11086 4000 Piedmont Parkway Suite 210 High Point, NC 27265

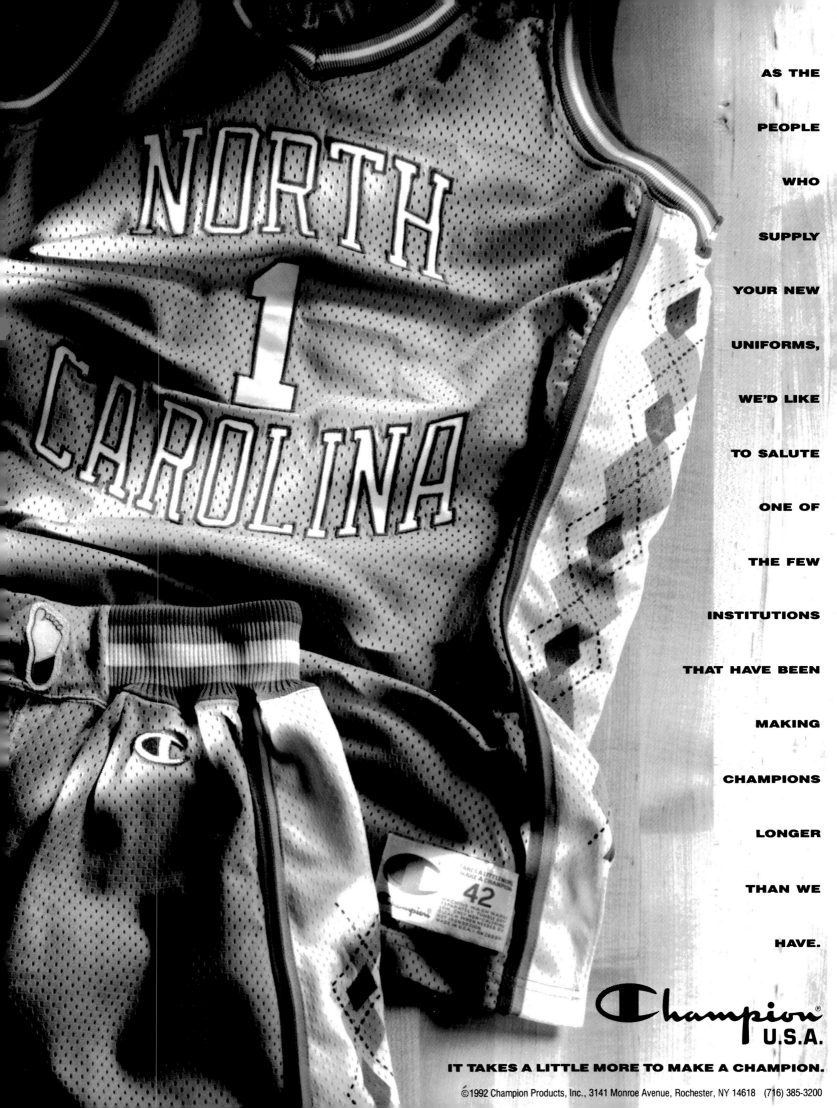

craftsmanship
commitment
creativity

TOOLS
OF THE
TRADE

THE HICKORY PRINTING GROUP

HICKORY HIGH POINT ICARD ASHEVILLE
GROUP HEADQUARTERS 1-704-322-3431

HUGH MORTON

The 1993 Tar Heels

00	Eric Montross	C	7-0	270	Jr.	Indianapolis, Ind.
3	Pat Sullivan	F	6-8	216	Jr.	Bogota, N.J.
4	Larry Davis	G	6-3	184	Fr.	Denmark, S.C.
5	Henrik Rodl	G	6-8	203	Sr.	Heusentamm, Ger.
11	Scott Cherry	G	6-5	180	Sr.	Ballston Spa, N.Y.
14	Derrick Phelps	G	6-4	181	Jr.	East Elmhurst, N.Y.
21	Donald Williams	G	6-3	194	So.	Garner, N.C.
24	Dante Calabria	G	6-4	186	Fr.	Beaver Falls, Pa.
31	Brian Reese	F	6-6	215	Jr.	Bronx, N.Y.
33	Kevin Salvadori	C-F	7-0	224	Jr.	Pittsburgh, Pa.
34	George Lynch	F	6-8	220	Sr.	Roanoke, Va.
35	Travis Stephenson	F	6-7	220	Sr.	Angier, N.C.
40	Ed Geth	F	6-9	250	Fr.	Norfolk, Va.
55	Matt Wenstrom	C	7-1	260	Sr.	Houston, Texas

1992-93 RESULTS AND STATISTICS

NORTH CAROLINA (34-4, 14-2 ACC)

DATE		RESULTS		LEADING SCORER	LEADING REBOUNDER	SITE	ATTEN.
Dec. 1	W	119-82	Old Dominion	Williams 21	Lynch 8	H	18,807 *
Dec. 4	W	108-67	South Carolina	Williams 23	Lynch 11	N-Charlotte, N.C.	17,804
Dec. 5	W	104-68	Texas	Williams 19	Montross 10	N-Charlotte, N.C.	16,931
Dec. 9	W	78-62	Virginia Tech	Montross 19	Lynch 11	A-Roanoke, Va.	8,554
Dec. 13	W	84-76	Houston	Williams 21	Lynch 8	H	20,605 *
Dec. 20	W	103-56	Butler	Lynch 18	Lynch 8	A	9,951
Dec. 22	W	84-64	Ohio State	Montross 20	Lynch 16	A	13,276 *
Dec. 28	W	80-59	Southwestern Louisiana	Lynch, Montross 17	Lynch 9	N-Honolulu, Ha.	7,634 *
Dec. 29	L	78-79	Michigan	Phelps 15	Lynch 16	N-Honolulu, Ha.	7,640 *
Dec. 30	W	101-84	Hawaii	Montross 28	Lynch 9	A	7,635 *
Jan. 4	W	98-60	Cornell	Phelps, Williams 16	Lynch 9	H	18,458
Jan. 7	W	100-67	N.C. State	Williams 23	Lynch, Montross 9	A	12,400 *
Jan. 9	W	101-73	Maryland	Williams 20	Montross 13	H	21,407 *
Jan. 13	W	80-67	Georgia Tech	Lynch, Phelps 20	Lynch 11	H	21,572 *
Jan. 16	W	82-72	Clemson	Lynch 17	Lynch 13	A	11,000 *
Jan. 20	W	80-58	Virginia	Salvadori 14	Lynch 11	H	21,572 *
Jan. 24	W	70-66	Seton Hall	Lynch 25	Lynch 7	A	20,029 *
Jan. 27	W	82-77	Florida State	Williams 19	Lynch 10	H	21,572 *
Jan. 30	L	62-88	Wake Forest	Reese 16	Lynch 9	A	14,475 *
Feb. 3	L	67-81	Duke	Montross 22	Montross 13	A	9,314 *
Feb. 6	W	104-58	N.C. State	Lynch 14	Montross 8	H	21,572 *
Feb. 9	W	77-63	Maryland	Montross 17	Lynch 12	A	14,500 *
Feb. 14	W	77-66	Georgia Tech	Williams 21	Montross 9	A	9,922 *
Feb. 17	W	80-67	Clemson	Montross 22	Montross 7	H	21,147 *
Feb. 21	W	78-58	Virginia	Lynch, Montross 17	Lynch 11	A	8,864 *
Feb. 23	W	85-56	Notre Dame	Montross 19	Lynch, Reese 8	H	21,572 *
Feb. 27	W	86-76	Florida State	Reese 25	Lynch 10	A	13,251 *
Mar. 3	W	83-65	Wake Forest	Lynch 18	Lynch, Salvadori 7	H	21,572 *
Mar. 7	W	83-69	Duke	Williams 27	Lynch 11	H	21,572 *
Mar. 12	W	102-66	Maryland	Lynch 22	Lynch 15	N-Charlotte, N.C.	23,532 *
Mar. 13	W	74-56	Virginia	Williams 19	Lynch 11	N-Charlotte, N.C.	23,532 *
Mar. 14	L	75-77	Georgia Tech	Reese 24	Montross 17	N-Charlotte, N.C.	23,532 *
Mar. 18	W	85-65	East Carolina	Montross 17	Montross 9	N-Winston-Salem, N.C.	14,366 *
Mar. 20	W	112-67	Rhode Island	Williams 17	Montross 9	N-Winston-Salem, N.C.	14,366 *
Mar. 26	W	80-74	Arkansas	Lynch 23	Lynch 10	N-East Rutherford, N.J.	19,761 *
Mar. 28	W	**75-68	Cincinnati	Lynch 21	Lynch 14	N-East Rutherford, N.J.	19,761 *
Apr. 3	W	78-68	Kansas	Williams 25	Lynch 10	N-New Orleans, La.	64,151 *
Apr. 5	W	77-71	Michigan	Williams 25	Lynch 10	N-New Orleans, La.	64,151 *

* Sellout
** Overtime

Player	G	GS	Min.	Avg.	FGM	FGA	Pct.	3PM	3PA	Pct.	FTM	FTA	Pct.	Off.	Def.	Tot.	Avg.	PF	DQ	A	TO	BS	ST	Pts.	Avg.
Eric Montross	38	36	1076	28.3	222	361	.615	0	0	.000	156	228	.684	126	164	290	7.6	113	3	28	67	47	23	600	15.8
George Lynch	38	37	1148	30.2	235	469	.501	2	11	.182	88	132	.667	138	227	365	9.6	85	3	72	89	21	89	560	14.7
Donald Williams	37	14	899	24.3	174	380	.458	83	199	.417	97	117	.829	20	51	71	1.9	52	0	46	40	2	38	528	14.3
Brian Reese	35	30	841	24.0	152	300	.507	22	60	.367	72	104	.692	58	67	125	3.6	34	0	83	82	7	24	398	11.4
Derrick Phelps	36	33	1011	28.1	111	243	.457	15	48	.313	56	83	.675	56	101	157	4.4	68	1	196	110	3	82	293	8.1
Pat Sullivan	38	8	633	16.7	88	170	.518	9	30	.300	60	76	.789	44	48	92	2.4	43	0	51	35	2	26	245	6.4
Kevin Salvadori	38	2	507	13.3	66	144	.458	0	0	.000	38	54	.704	61	77	138	3.6	79	2	12	24	46	8	170	4.5
Henrick Rödl	38	26	740	19.5	58	117	.496	22	62	.355	25	38	.658	11	46	57	1.5	50	0	136	60	10	39	163	4.3
Matt Wenstrom	33	1	166	5.0	34	61	.557	0	1	.000	16	27	.593	17	30	47	1.4	17	0	7	13	6	1	84	2.5
Ed Geth	21	0	67	3.2	16	25	.640	0	0	.000	12	17	.706	12	16	28	1.3	14	0	0	7	0	4	44	2.1
Larry Davis	21	0	74	3.5	14	40	.350	2	9	.222	14	23	.609	6	10	16	0.8	4	0	4	5	0	6	44	2.1
Scott Cherry	33	2	160	4.8	20	33	.606	4	8	.500	25	35	.714	4	19	23	0.7	15	0	30	21	1	9	69	2.1
Dante Calabria	35	0	250	7.1	24	52	.462	9	23	.391	7	9	.778	5	22	27	0.8	26	1	29	21	1	8	64	1.8
Travis Stephenson	21	1	52	2.5	5	11	.455	0	1	.000	0	0	.000	3	3	6	0.3	1	0	3	4	0	0	10	0.5
Pearce Landry	1	0	1	1.0	0	1	.000	0	0	.000	0	0	.000	1	0	1	1.0	1	0	1	0	0	1	0	0.0
Team																118									
North Carolina	38		7625		1219	2407	.506	168	452	.372	666	943	.706	562	881	1561	41.1	602	10	698	580	146	358	3272	86.1
Opponents	38		7625		978	2370	.413	235	716	.328	405	603	.672	518	704	1222	32.2	746	20	538	687	138	273	2596	68.3

Score By Halves	1	2	OT	Total	Deadball Rebounds
Opponents	1213	1381	2	2596	124
North Carolina	1544	1719	9	3272	148

1992-93 GAME-BY-GAME BOX SCORES

NORTH CAROLINA 119 / OLD DOMINION 82

NORTH CAROLINA 119
OLD DOMINION 82

TUESDAY, DECEMBER 1, 1992
SMITH CENTER, CHAPEL HILL, N.C.
(ATTENDANCE: 18,807)

Old Dominion	FG	FT	REB	A	PF	TP
Sessoms	4-14	10-10	8	0	4	20
Mullen	5-8	2-3	4	1	1	12
Hodge	2-4	0-2	1	0	3	4
Swann	4-12	4-4	2	3	1	14
Jackson	4-17	2-2	7	2	2	13
Anderson	3-8	3-4	0	2	1	9
Harvey	1-6	0-4	4	1	4	2
A. Wright	0-1	0-2	1	1	3	0
Jones	1-5	1-2	1	0	2	3
Larkin	1-4	0-0	1	0	3	2
W. Wright	1-1	0-0	2	0	0	3
Totals	**26-80**	**22-33**	**38**	**10**	**24**	**82**

North Carolina	FG	FT	REB	A	PF	TP
Reese	8-8	2-5	3	4	1	19
Lynch	5-8	2-4	8	6	1	12
Montross	8-8	4-4	5	1	2	20
Williams	5-8	9-10	2	3	1	21
Rodl	2-3	0-0	2	11	3	5
Calabria	0-2	0-0	0	0	5	0
Sullivan	6-9	5-6	4	1	2	18
Cherry	1-1	0-0	1	2	0	2
Salvadoi	3-4	1-2	5	0	3	7
Wenstrom	1-1	1-2	4	0	1	3
Davis	1-1	4-4	1	2	0	6
Stephenson	0-1	0-0	0	1	0	0
Geth	3-3	0-0	1	0	1	6
Totals	**43-57**	**28-37**	**36**	**31**	**20**	**119**

Old Dominion	41	41	—	82
North Carolina	54	65	—	119

Turnovers: Old Dominion 23 (Swann 6); North Carolina 22 (Reese 4)
Blocked Shots: Old Dominion 1 (Mullen); UNC 7 (Salvadori 3)
Steals: Old Dominion 9 (Mullen, Swann, Anderson 2); UNC 18 (Lynch, Rodl 4)
Field Goal Pct.: Old Dominion .325; UNC .754
Free Throw Pct.: Old Dominion .667; UNC .757
Three-Point Field Goal Pct.: Old Dominion .250; UNC .455
Three-Point Field Goal Shooting: Old Dominino (Sessoms 2-7, Mullen 0-1, Swann 2-4, Jackson 3-11, Anderson 0-2, Jones 0-3, Larkin 0-3, W. Wright 1-1); UNC (Reese 1-1, Williams 2-4, Rodl 1-2, Calabria 0-2, Sullivan 1-2)
Technical Fouls: None
Officials: Gordon, Kersey, Upton

NORTH CAROLINA 108 / SOUTH CAROLINA 67

NORTH CAROLINA 108
SOUTH CAROLINA 67

FRIDAY, DECEMBER 4, 1992
CHARLOTTE COLISEUM, CHARLOTTE, N.C.
(ATTENDANCE: 17,804)

South Carolina	FG	FT	REB	A	PF	TP
Hall	7-11	2-5	3	2	4	16
Watson	5-14	2-3	2	1	2	12
Ignjatovic	2-5	0-0	3	0	0	5
Rich	1-2	0-0	2	8	2	2
Bynum	0-6	0-0	2	2	1	0
Franklin	5-11	0-0	1	1	0	13
McKoy	2-4	0-0	5	0	2	4
Hoskins	4-7	0-0	2	0	1	9
Wilson	1-4	4-6	4	0	3	6
Leso	0-1	0-0	1	1	0	0
Totals	**27-65**	**8-14**	**28**	**15**	**15**	**67**

North Carolina	FG	FT	REB	A	PF	TP
Reese	4-8	2-2	2	3	1	11
Lynch	7-14	4-5	11	0	3	18
Montross	7-11	2-2	9	0	2	16
Rodl	1-3	0-0	2	3	2	3
Phelps	0-3	2-2	4	8	1	2
Sullivan	2-4	1-1	1	2	1	5
Davis	1-1	0-0	1	0	0	3
Cherry	2-2	0-0	0	4	0	4
Wliams	8-12	2-2	2	0	0	23
Calabria	2-2	0-0	3	2	0	5
Salvadori	3-4	2-2	0	0	2	8
Stephenson	1-1	0-0	0	0	0	2
Geth	1-2	2-2	1	0	1	4
Wenstrom	2-4	0-0	2	1	0	4
Totals	**41-71**	**17-18**	**44**	**23**	**13**	**108**

South Carolina	34	33	—	67
North Carolina	49	59	—	108

Turnovers: South Carolina 21 (Rich 4); UNC 18 (Reese 5)
Blocked Shots: South Carolina 7 (Wilson 3); UNC 5 (Montross 3)
Steals: South Carolina 7 (Ignjatovic 3); UNC 3 (Reese, Cherry, Williams 1)
Field Goal Pct.: South Carolina .415; UNC .577
Free Throw Pct.: South Carolina .571; UNC .944
Three-Point Field Goal Pct.: South Carolina .333; UNC .500
Three-Point Field Goal Shooting: South Carolina (Watson 0-1, Ignjatovic 1-2, Bynum 0-3, Franklin 3-6, Hoskins 1-3); UNC (Reese 1-2, Lynch 0-1, Rodl 1-3, Phelps 0-1, Sullivan 0-1, Davis 1-1, Williams 5-8, Calabria 1-1)
Technical Fouls: None
Officials: Herring, Croft, Steed

NORTH CAROLINA 104 / TEXAS 68

NORTH CAROLINA 104
TEXAS 68

SATURDAY, DECEMBER 5, 1992
CHARLOTTE COLISEUM, CHARLOTTE, N.C.
(ATTENDANCE: 16,931)

Texas	FG	FT	REB	A	PF	TP
Richardson	8-27	2-2	10	2	4	20
Houston	2-9	0-2	10	1	4	4
Burditt	6-13	0-5	19	1	3	12
Tyler	5-15	1-3	3	4	3	13
Rencher	3-21	2-5	2	0	2	9
Quarles	0-1	0-0	1	1	2	0
Hill	1-2	0-1	1	0	1	2
Watson	3-10	0-0	5	1	2	8
Chaplin	0-0	0-0	0	0	1	0
Totals	**28-98**	**5-18**	**55**	**10**	**22**	**68**

North Carolina	FG	FT	REB	A	PF	TP
Reese	4-4	0-0	4	1	0	8
Lynch	7-14	3-5	7	3	2	17
Montross	5-11	4-4	10	2	3	14
Rodl	3-3	0-0	1	3	2	7
Phelps	1-2	2-2	4	3	4	5
Sullivan	3-9	2-3	6	1	0	9
Davis	1-4	0-2	1	0	0	2
Cherry	2-3	0-4	2	2	1	4
Williams	6-7	4-5	1	3	0	19
Calabria	3-3	0-0	0	2	0	7
Salvadori	2-4	0-1	4	0	3	4
Stephenson	0-1	0-0	3	0	0	0
Geth	0-1	3-4	2	0	1	3
Wenstrom	2-5	1-2	6	1	2	5
Totals	**39-71**	**19-32**	**62**	**21**	**18**	**104**

Texas	31	37	—	68
North Carolina	61	43	—	104

Turnovers: Texas 13 (Tyler, Rencher 5); UNC 21 (Rodl 4)
Blocked Shots: Texas 5 (Burditt 2); UNC 4 (Salvadori 3)
Steals: Texas 7 (Burditt, Watson 2); UNC 7 (Lynch 4)
Field Goal Pct.: Texas .286 UNC .549
Free Throw Pct.: Texas .278; UNC .594
Three-Point Field Goal Pct.: Texas .212; UNC .875
Three-Point Field Goal Shooting: Texas (Richardson 2-5, Tyler 2-11, Rencher 1-9, Hill 0-1, Watson 2-7); UNC (Rodl 1-1, Phelps 1-1, Sullivan 1-1, Davis 0-1, Williams 3-3, Calabria 1-1)
Technical Fouls: None
Officials: Wirtz, Moreau, Gordon

HUGH MORTON

This message rang true throughout the NCAA Tournament, as the Tar Heels knocked off six opponents on their way to a second national championship under Coach Dean Smith.

NORTH CAROLINA	78
VIRGINIA TECH	62

WEDNESDAY, DECEMBER 9, 1992
ROANOKE CIVIC CENTER, ROANOKE VA.
(ATTENDANCE: 8,554)

North Carolina	FG	FT	REB	A	PF	TP
Lynch	8-13	2-2	11	3	4	18
Sullivan	3-7	1-2	5	5	1	8
Montross	7-14	5-6	10	1	2	19
Phelps	0-7	2-2	8	2	0	2
Rodl	3-6	3-3	3	4	2	9
Salvadori	2-5	2-3	3	1	3	6
Cherry	2-3	4-4	0	1	0	9
Calabria	2-2	0-0	2	1	1	5
Wenstrom	0-0	1-2	1	0	3	1
Davis	0-1	0-0	0	0	1	0
Geth	0-1	1-2	2	0	0	1
Stephenson	0-0	0-0	0	0	0	0
Totals	27-59	21-26	49	18	17	78

Virginia Tech	FG	FT	REB	A	PF	TP
Jackson	9-17	0-0	6	2	3	21
Elliott	4-10	1-3	5	0	1	9
Careuth	3-8	0-1	2	2	4	6
Purcell	2-7	1-1	2	5	2	5
Good	1-4	0-2	2	0	2	2
Corker	0-1	0-0	2	1	0	0
Watlington	1-8	0-0	4	2	3	3
Jackson	0-1	2-2	0	1	2	2
Hall	2-2	0-2	1	0	0	6
Smith	3-6	2-2	2	1	2	8
Totals	25-64	6-13	28	14	19	62

North Carolina	41	37 — 78
Virginia Tech	26	36 — 62

Turnovers: UNC 18 (Phelps, Rodl 5); Virginia Tech 14 (Purcell 4)
Blocked Shots: UNC 4 (Salvadori 2); Virginia Tech 4 (Careuth 3)
Steals: UNC 3 (Sullivan, Rodl, Cherry 1); Virginia Tech 3 (Elliott, Careuth, Purcell 1)
Field Goal Pct.: UNC .458; Virginia Tech .391
Free Throw Pct.: UNC .808; Virginia Tech .462
Three-Point Field Goal Pct.: UNC .333; Virginia Tech .400
Three-Point Field Goal Shooting: UNC (Sullivan 1-3, Phelps 0-3, Rodl 0-1, Cherry 1-1, Calabria 1-1); Virginia Tech (Jackson 3-6, Elliott 0-2, Purcell 0-2, Watlington 1-3, Hall 2-2)
Technical Fouls: None
Officials: Wirtz, Rose, Herring

NORTH CAROLINA	84
HOUSTON	76

SUNDAY, DECEMBER 13, 1992
SMITH CENTER, CHAPEL HILL, N.C.
(ATTENDANCE: 20,605)
ACC-BIG EAST CHALLENGE

Houston	FG	FT	REB	A	PF	TP
Smith	4-9	1-2	2	0	1	10
Drain	2-7	0-0	1	2	3	6
Outlaw	3-3	3-6	8	1	3	9
Diaz	4-12	8-9	5	0	4	17
Goldwire	9-14	3-5	0	5	2	22
Carrasco	0-2	0-0	5	0	1	0
Evans	4-8	0-0	1	2	3	12
Wiles	0-1	0-0	0	0	0	0
Totals	26-56	15-22	23	10	17	76

North Carolina	FG	FT	REB	A	PF	TP
Sullivan	6-7	0-0	1	1	3	13
Lynch	6-12	1-2	8	3	2	13
Montross	6-6	3-9	7	0	3	15
Rodl	2-4	0-0	4	8	2	5
Phelps	3-5	3-4	7	12	3	9
Calabria	1-2	0-0	0	0	1	2
Williams	7-12	3-4	0	0	3	21
Wenstrom	1-1	0-0	0	0	1	2
Salvadori	2-6	0-0	4	1	3	4
Totals	34-55	10-19	34	25	21	84

Houston	36	40 — 76
North Carolina	42	42 — 84

Turnovers: Houston 23 (Goldwire 9); UNC 25 (Lynch 9)
Blocked Shots: Houston 0; UNC 2 (Lynch, Salvadori 1)
Steals: Houston 12 (Drain 3); UNC 10 (Phelps 7)
Field Goal Pct.: Houston .464; UNC .618
Free Throw Pct.: Houston .681; UNC .526
Three-Point Field Goal Pct.: Houston .391; UNC .462
Three-Point Field Goal Shooting: Houston (Smith 1-2, Drain 2-5, Diaz 1-7, Goldwire 1-2, Evans 4-7); UNC (Sullivan 1-1, Rodl 1-2, Phelps 0-1, Calabria 0-1, Williams 4-8)
Technical Fouls: None
Officials: McDaniel, Shortnacy, Armstrong

NORTH CAROLINA	103
BUTLER	56

SUNDAY, DECEMBER 20, 1992
HINKLE FIELD HOUSE, INDIANAPOLIS, IND.
(ATTENDANCE: 9,951)

North Carolina	FG	FT	REB	A	PF	TP
Sullivan	2-3	0-0	2	1	0	4
Lynch	8-16	2-3	8	2	1	18
Montross	6-13	1-3	7	1	4	13
Rodl	3-5	2-4	0	3	2	10
Phelps	2-2	0-0	3	9	3	4
Davis	0-3	0-0	1	1	0	0
Cherry	0-0	2-2	1	3	2	2
Williams	4-6	2-2	2	1	0	12
Calabria	3-3	0-0	1	3	1	8
Reese	3-6	3-3	6	2	2	10
Salvadori	3-4	0-0	3	0	1	6
Stephenson	1-1	0-0	1	0	0	2
Geth	1-1	0-2	3	0	2	2
Wenstrom	4-8	4-7	3	1	0	1
Totals	40-71	16-26	43	27	18	103

Butler	FG	FT	REB	A	PF	TP
Reliford	2-5	2-4	2	1	3	6
Beauford	5-15	2-3	7	1	4	14
Brens	2-3	0-0	5	0	4	4
Bowen	0-5	0-0	1	4	2	0
Guice	6-18	0-1	4	0	3	13
Bowens	2-4	0-0	0	2	1	4
Taylor	3-9	0-0	8	2	2	6
McKenzie	1-6	1-2	3	0	2	3
Allen	1-2	0-0	1	0	2	2
Miskel	2-5	0-2	4	0	2	4
Phillips	0-0	0-0	0	0	0	0
Totals	24-72	5-12	39	10	25	56

North Carolina	50	53 —103
Butler	26	30 — 56

Turnovers: UNC 16 (Phelps 6); Butler 26 (Bowen 5)
Blocked Shots: UNC 2 (Lynch, Montross 1); Butler 0
Steals: UNC 5 (Lynch, Rodl 2); Butler 7 (Guice 3)
Field Goal Pct.: UNC .563; Butler .333
Free Throw Pct.: UNC .615; Butler .417
Three-Point Field Goal Pct.: UNC .538; Butler .130
Three-Point Field Goal Shooting: UNC (Sullivan 0-1, Lynch 0-2, Rodl 2-4, Williams 2-3, Calabria 2-2, Reese 1-1); Butler (Beauford 2-4, Bowen 0-3, Guice 1-9, Bowens 0-1, McKenzie 0-4, Allen 0-1, Miskel 0-1)
Technical Fouls: None
Officials: Rose, Gray, Wood

HUGH MORTON

This Tar Heel fan obviously enjoyed the prospects of UNC playing in the NCAAs after two-time defending champion Duke had been eliminated.

NORTH CAROLINA 84 — OHIO STATE 64

TUESDAY, DECEMBER 22, 1992
ST. JOHN ARENA, COLUMBUS, OHIO
(ATTENDANCE: 13,276)

North Carolina	FG	FT	REB	A	PF	TP
Montross	8-8	4-8	9	0	1	20
Sullivan	3-5	0-0	2	2	1	6
Rodl	2-2	0-0	2	4	2	4
Cherry	1-1	0-0	0	0	0	2
Phelps	4-12	6-9	2	4	1	14
Williams	4-8	0-0	1	1	1	9
Calabria	0-0	0-0	2	1	0	0
Reese	7-11	0-1	2	1	1	14
Salvadori	1-1	2-2	4	0	3	4
Lynch	5-12	1-2	16	3	3	11
Wenstrom	0-0	0-0	0	1	0	0
Totals	35-60	13-22	42	17	13	84

Ohio State	FG	FT	REB	A	PF	TP
Simpson	4-11	0-0	0	1	4	9
Etzler	3-6	0-0	0	2	1	7
Skelton	5-11	2-2	1	2	1	15
Davis	2-6	0-0	4	8	1	5
Brandewie	1-4	0-0	2	2	2	2
Macon	2-4	0-1	0	0	1	4
Funderburke	7-9	3-5	6	2	2	17
Dudley	1-3	0-0	4	1	4	2
Watson	0-0	0-0	0	0	1	0
Ratliff	1-5	1-2	4	0	2	3
Wilbourne	0-0	0-0	0	0	0	0
Totals	26-59	6-10	24	18	19	64

North Carolina	35	49 —	84
Ohio State	38	26 —	64

Turnovers: UNC 17 (Phelps 5); Ohio State 18 (Etzler 4)
Blocked Shots: UNC 1 (Montross); Ohio State 1 (Macon)
Steals: UNC 8 (Phelps 3); Ohio State 3 (Davis, Brandewie, Dudley)
Field Goal Pct.: UNC .583; Ohio State .441
Free Throw Pct.: UNC .591; Ohio State .600
Three-Point Field Goal Pct.: UNC .200; Ohio State .286
Three-Point Field Goal Shooting: North Carolina (Sullivan 0-1, Phelps 0-1, Williams 1-2, Lynch 0-1); Ohio State (Simpson 1-4, Etzler 1-3, Skelton 3-7, Davis 1-4, Macon 0-1, Ratliff 0-2)
Technical Fouls: None
Officials: Paparo, Edsall, Pitts

NORTH CAROLINA 80 — SW LOUISIANA 59

MONDAY, DECEMBER 28, 1992
NEAL BLAISDELL ARENA, HONOLULU, HAWAII
(ATTENDANCE: 7,634)

North Carolina	FG	FT	REB	A	PF	TP
Montross	7-10	3-5	6	1	3	17
Sullivan	4-6	2-2	5	2	0	10
Rodl	4-6	0-3	3	3	1	9
Cherry	0-0	2-2	0	0	1	2
Phelps	4-6	0-0	5	6	3	10
Williams	2-11	3-3	2	2	1	7
Calabria	1-2	0-0	2	0	2	2
Reese	2-8	0-2	3	2	0	4
Salvadori	1-6	0-0	5	0	2	2
Lynch	8-17	1-2	9	0	2	17
Stephenson	0-0	0-0	0	0	0	0
Geth	0-0	0-0	0	0	0	0
Wenstrom	0-0	0-0	1	1	0	0
Totals	33-72	11-19	44	17	15	80

SW Louisiana	FG	FT	REB	A	PF	TP
Allen	7-22	1-2	1	4	3	17
Starks	7-14	1-2	8	3	4	15
Moore	0-5	0-0	0	0	0	0
Hill	5-13	0-0	9	0	3	11
Griggs	1-1	0-0	1	0	1	2
Mackyeon	3-4	0-1	7	1	4	6
Collins	2-4	0-2	6	0	3	4
Boudreaux	2-4	0-0	1	1	4	4
Totals	27-67	2-7	34	9	22	59

North Carolina	31	49 —	80
SW Louisiana	30	29 —	59

Turnovers: UNC 15 (Montross, Sullivan, Phelps 3); SW La. 20 (Allen 5)
Blocked Shots: UNC 1 (Salvadori); SW La. 3 (Starks, Griggs, Mackyeon)
Steals: UNC 13 (Lynch 5); SW La. 8 (Collins 4)
Field Goal Pct.: UNC .458; SW La. .403
Free Throw Pct.: UNC .579; SW La. .286
Three-Point Field Goal Pct.: UNC .200; SW La. .214
Three-Point Field Goal Shooting: UNC (Sullivan 0-1, Rodl 1-2, Phelps 2-3, Williams 0-6, Reese 0-2, Lynch 0-1); SW La. (Allen 2-11, Moore 0-1, Hill 1-2)
Technical Fouls: None
Officials: Hightower, Shapiro, Hernandez

MICHIGAN 79 — NORTH CAROLINA 78

TUESDAY, DECEMBER 29, 1992
NEAL BLAISDELL ARENA, HONOLULU, HAWAII
(ATTENDANCE: 7,640)

Michigan	FG	FT	REB	A	PF	TP
Pelinka	2-6	0-0	3	0	2	5
Webber	10-17	5-6	8	4	3	27
Rose	7-14	7-9	5	2	2	22
Fife	0-0	1-2	2	1	2	1
Talley	0-0	0-0	0	1	2	0
Jackson	0-1	0-0	0	0	0	0
King	3-7	0-2	3	6	3	6
Howard	4-7	1-2	7	0	3	9
Voskuil	1-5	0-0	1	0	0	2
Riley	3-3	1-1	4	0	1	7
Totals	30-60	15-22	34	14	18	79

North Carolina	FG	FT	REB	A	PF	TP
Montross	5-8	4-6	10	2	2	14
Sullivan	1-4	2-4	3	0	1	4
Rodl	3-3	0-0	1	3	3	7
Phelps	4-11	5-7	0	3	1	15
Williams	4-8	4-4	1	1	2	13
Calabria	1-2	0-0	1	1	0	3
Reese	4-4	2-2	3	1	2	10
Salvadori	0-0	0-0	0	2	5	0
Lynch	5-18	2-4	16	0	1	12
Totals	27-58	19-27	37	13	17	78

Michigan	40	39 —	79
North Carolina	36	42 —	78

Turnovers: Michigan 17 (Rose, Howard 6); UNC 19 (Reese 7)
Blocked Shots: Michigan 7 (Webber 5); UNC 3 (Montross 2)
Steals: Michigan 4 (King 2); UNC 10 (Phelps 6)
Field Goal Pct.: Michigan .500; UNC .466
Free Throw Pct.: Michigan .682; UNC .704
Three-Point Field Goal Pct.: Michigan .250; UNC .385
Three-Point Field Goal Shooting: Michigan (Pelinka 1-5, Webber 2-3, Rose 1-3, King 0-2, Voskuil 0-3); UNC (Sullivan 0-1, Rodl 1-1, Phelps 2-6, Williams 1-4, Calabria 1-1)
Technical Fouls: Webber
Officials: Hall, Shapiro, Hernandez

HUGH MORTON

A familiar sight for North Carolina fans: the Tar Heels huddle before the start of an NCAA Tournament game.

NORTH CAROLINA 101 — HAWAII 84

WEDNESDAY, DECEMBER 30, 1992
NEAL BLAISDELL ARENA, HONOLULU, HAWAII.
(ATTENDANCE: 7,635)

Hawaii	FG	FT	REB	A	PF	TP
Washington	0-1	0-0	0	0	0	0
Ribeiro	5-9	5-6	1	1	4	17
Akana	8-11	0-0	3	5	2	18
Winter	1-1	0-0	0	0	0	2
Taylor	0-1	0-0	0	0	0	0
McGee	3-4	0-1	2	7	3	6
Ruffin	3-8	2-2	0	2	2	8
Phillip	3-4	6-9	6	1	4	12
Holmes	0-0	0-0	0	0	0	0
Shepherd	4-8	1-2	4	1	2	9
Walz	5-13	0-0	7	3	5	12
Totals	32-60	14-20	25	20	22	84

North Carolina	FG	FT	REB	A	PF	TP
Montross	9-15	10-14	7	1	4	28
Sullivan	2-3	4-4	2	3	0	8
Rodl	1-2	1-1	2	4	1	3
Cherry	1-1	0-0	1	0	1	2
Phelps	1-6	1-2	2	6	1	3
Williams	5-7	4-6	1	1	2	17
Calabria	1-3	0-0	1	1	2	2
Reese	2-5	4-4	5	2	1	8
Salvadori	3-4	0-0	1	1	2	6
Lynch	8-12	3-4	9	1	2	19
Stephenson	0-0	0-0	0	0	0	0
Geth	0-0	0-0	0	0	1	0
Wenstrom	2-3	1-2	2	0	1	5
Totals	35-61	28-37	36	20	18	101

Hawaii	34	50	— 84
North Carolina	51	50	—101

Turnovers: Hawaii 14 (Shepherd 4); UNC 10 (Phelps 4)
Blocked Shots: Hawaii 5 (Phillip 2); UNC 3 (Montross, Salvadori, Lynch)
Steals: Hawaii 3 (Walls 2); UNC 7 (Rodl 2)
Field Goal Pct.: Hawaii .533; UNC .574
Free Throw Pct.: Hawaii .700; UNC .757
Three-Point Field Goal Pct.: Hawaii .429; UNC .600
Three-Point Field Goal Shooting: Hawaii (Ribeiro 2-3, Akana 2-5, Ruffin 0-2, Walls 2-4); UNC (Rodl 0-1, Phelps 0-1, Williams 3-3)
Technical Fouls: Montross
Officials: Reynolds, Sternberger, Tanibe

NORTH CAROLINA 98 — CORNELL 60

MONDAY, JANUARY 4, 1993
SMITH CENTER, CHAPEL HILL, N.C.
(ATTENDANCE: 18,458)

Cornell	FG	FT	REB	A	PF	TP
Marshall	5-12	2-5	7	0	3	12
Kopf	1-4	0-0	3	0	4	2
Treadwell	4-6	0-0	5	0	4	8
Gaca	4-14	0-0	1	3	1	11
Parker	3-6	0-0	1	5	0	6
Ableson	0-4	2-2	1	3	1	2
Whitehead	5-12	2-2	5	2	4	12
Maurer	0-0	0-0	1	0	1	0
Escarzega	0-0	0-0	1	0	2	0
Beck	1-1	0-0	0	0	0	2
Schuckman	1-1	0-0	0	0	0	3
Tolliver	1-1	0-0	0	0	0	2
Hayes	0-0	0-0	0	0	0	0
Meakem	0-0	0-0	0	0	0	0
Nash	0-0	0-0	0	0	0	0
Totals	25-61	6-9	30	13	20	60

North Carolina	FG	FT	REB	A	PF	TP
Reese	5-7	2-2	2	1	1	14
Salvadori	3-7	1-2	8	0	3	7
Montross	2-6	3-5	6	0	3	7
Rodl	0-2	0-0	3	3	0	0
Phelps	8-14	0-1	6	6	1	16
Sullivan	3-5	3-5	4	0	0	9
Williams	6-10	1-2	3	2	0	16
Lynch	6-11	1-3	9	3	2	13
Calabria	2-3	0-0	0	1	0	4
Wenstrom	3-3	0-0	1	0	1	6
Cherry	0-2	2-2	1	3	2	2
Stephenson	0-1	0-0	0	0	0	0
Geth	1-1	2-2	2	0	0	4
Totals	39-72	15-24	46	19	13	98

Cornell	28	32	— 60
North Carolina	47	51	— 98

Turnovers: Cornell 25 (Marshall 7); UNC 14 (Lynch 3)
Blocked Shots: Cornell 2 (Treadwell, Whitehead); UNC 9 (Rodl 3)
Steals: Cornell 8 (Parker 3); UNC 18 (Phelps 7)
Field Goal Pct.: Cornell .410; UNC .542
Free Throw Pct.: Cornell .667; UNC .625
Three-Point Field Goal Pct.: Cornell .364; UNC .625
Three-Point Field Goal Shooting: Cornell (Gaca 3-8, Ableson 0-1, Whitehead 0-1, Schuckman 1-1); UNC (Reese 2-2, Williams 3-5, Cherry 0-1)
Technical Fouls: None
Officials: Allen, Nobles, Styons

NORTH CAROLINA 100 — N.C. STATE 67

THURSDAY, JANUARY 7, 1993
REYNOLDS COLISEUM, RALEGH, N.C.
(ATTENDANCE: 12,400)

North Carolina	FG	FT	REB	A	PF	TP
Reese	4-6	2-2	3	4	1	11
Lynch	8-16	5-7	9	2	2	21
Montross	4-7	3-5	9	1	4	11
Rodl	1-4	0-0	3	3	2	3
Phelps	4-10	0-0	7	5	1	8
Williams	7-11	4-5	4	2	2	23
Sullivan	4-5	0-0	2	1	0	8
Salvadori	0-3	3-4	2	1	5	3
Calabria	0-1	2-2	2	2	1	2
Cherry	1-2	2-2	2	1	2	4
Wenstrom	0-0	0-0	0	0	0	0
Geth	1-3	0-0	2	0	2	2
Davis	1-1	2-4	0	0	0	4
Stephenson	0-0	0-0	0	0	0	0
Totals	35-69	23-31	49	22	22	100

N.C. State	FG	FT	REB	A	PF	TP
Davis	3-10	1-2	5	0	5	8
Bakalli	4-12	4-7	4	2	1	14
Thompson	2-6	7-8	4	1	4	11
McCuller	2-7	1-2	1	2	0	5
Marshall	3-10	0-0	5	4	2	9
Wilson	3-4	0-0	0	0	5	7
Newman	1-4	0-0	0	1	4	2
Fuller	1-2	1-3	3	0	3	3
Lewis	1-2	4-4	3	0	1	8
Totals	21-57	18-26	29	10	25	67

North Carolina	51	49	—100
N.C State	30	37	— 67

Turnovers: UNC 13 (Rodl 3); N.C. State 15 (Marshall 5)
Blocked Shots: UNC 2 (Montross, Rodl); N.C. State 0
Steals: UNC 8 (Lynch 6); N.C. State 9 (Thompson, Marshall, Wilson 2)
Field Goal Pct.: UNC .507; N.C. State .368
Free Throw Pct.: UNC .742; N.C. State .692
Three-Point Field Goal Pct.: UNC .467; N.C. State .259
Three-Point Field Goal Shooting: North Carolina (Reese 1-2, Rodl 1-2, Phelps 0-2, Williams 5-8, Cherry 0-1); N.C. State (Davis 1-4, Bakalli 2-9, McCuller 0-4, Marshall 3-7, Wilson 1-1, Newman 0-2)
Technical Fouls: None
Officials: Mareau, Gray, Gordon

HUGH MORTON

The late Jim Valvano, seen here with Brent Musberger, made his last public appearance at the Smith Center for the broadcast of the Duke game on March 7.

NORTH CAROLINA 101 / MARYLAND 73

SATURDAY, JANUARY 9, 1993
SMITH CENTER, CHAPEL HILL, N.C.
(ATTENDANCE: 21,407)

Maryland	FG	FT	REB	A	PF	TP
Hipp	2-5	1-2	1	2	4	6
Burns	7-17	0-0	7	2	3	14
Kerwin	3-5	0-2	2	0	3	6
Rhodes	6-15	0-0	3	2	3	13
McClinton	8-15	5-5	5	6	1	21
Walsh	0-2	2-2	1	1	3	2
Simpkins	2-5	0-0	3	2	1	4
Lucas	1-4	2-2	1	1	0	4
Bristol	0-0	0-0	0	0	0	0
Petrovic	0-0	0-0	0	0	1	0
Shultz	0-1	0-0	2	0	0	0
Thibeault	1-3	0-0	3	0	0	3
Totals	30-72	10-13	30	16	19	73

North Carolina	FG	FT	REB	A	PF	TP
Reese	3-6	0-2	3	2	1	6
Lynch	7-11	2-4	8	4	2	16
Montross	6-9	5-8	13	1	3	17
Rodl	1-2	0-0	0	4	0	3
Phelps	3-12	4-5	7	6	3	10
Sullivan	4-5	0-0	6	3	0	8
Williams	7-13	1-2	3	4	1	20
Salvadori	3-4	2-2	5	0	3	8
Calabria	1-1	2-2	1	1	1	5
Wenstrom	1-2	0-0	2	0	0	2
Cherry	1-1	0-2	0	0	0	2
Davis	1-2	0-0	0	0	0	2
Stephenson	0-1	0-0	0	0	0	0
Geth	1-1	0-0	1	0	0	2
Totals	39-70	16-27	50	25	14	101

Maryland	31	42 — 73
North Carolina	53	48 —101

Turnovers: Maryland 23 (Rhodes 7); UNC 23 (Lynch, Phelps 6)
Blocked Shots: Maryland 4 (Burns, Kerwin, Rhodes, Bristol); UNC 12 (Salvadori 6)
Steals: Maryland 12 (McLinton 3); UNC 12 (Lynch 3)
Field Goal Pct.: Maryland .417; UNC .557
Free Throw Pct.: Maryland .769; UNC .593
Three-Point Field Goal Pct.: Maryland .200; UNC .467
Three-Point Field Goal Shooting: Maryland (Hipp 1-2, Rhodes 1-8, McLinton 0-1, Walsh 0-1, Simpkins 0-1, Thibeault 1-2); UNC (Reese 0-1, Rodl 1-2, Phelps 0-2, Sullivan 0-1, Williams 5-8, Calabria 1-1)
Technical Fouls: None
Officials: Moreau, Edsall, Croft

NORTH CAROLINA 80 / GEORGIA TECH 67

WEDNESDAY, JANUARY 13, 1993
SMITH CENTER, CHAPEL HILL, N.C.
(ATTENDANCE: 21,572)

Georgia Tech	FG	FT	REB	A	PF	TP
Forrest	4-10	1-2	8	0	4	9
Mackey	5-9	2-3	7	1	4	12
Newbill	0-2	1-3	1	0	1	1
Moore	5-10	0-0	1	2	2	11
Best	8-14	0-0	2	6	1	20
Barry	1-4	0-0	5	5	1	2
Hill	5-7	0-0	0	0	2	12
Barnes	0-0	0-0	0	0	0	0
Totals	28-56	4-8	26	14	15	67

North Carolina	FG	FT	REB	A	PF	TP
Reese	7-13	0-0	1	2	1	15
Lynch	9-13	2-3	11	1	3	20
Montross	6-10	3-4	6	0	3	15
Rodl	0-2	0-0	1	5	0	0
Phelps	7-8	5-5	4	6	0	20
Sullivan	1-2	0-0	1	3	1	2
Williams	3-8	0-1	1	1	0	6
Calabria	0-0	0-0	0	1	1	0
Salvadori	0-3	0-1	3	0	2	0
Wenstrom	1-1	0-0	0	0	0	2
Cherry	0-0	0-0	0	0	0	0
Totals	34-60	10-14	30	19	11	80

Georgia Tech	34	33 — 67
North Carolina	39	41 — 80

Turnovers: Georgia Tech 18 (Mackey 6); UNC 14 (Lynch, Rodl 3)
Blocked Shots: Georgia Tech 2 (Forrest, Mackey); UNC 3 (Montross 2)
Steals: Georgia Tech 8 (Best 4); UNC 11 (Lynch 3)
Field Goal Pct.: Georgia Tech .500; UNC .567
Free Throw Pct.: Georgia Tech .500; UNC .714
Three-Point Field Goal Pct.: Georgia Tech .467; UNC .333
Three-Point Field Goal Shooting: Georgia Tech (Moore 1-4, Best 4-7, Barry 0-2, Hill 2-2); UNC (Reese 1-3, Rodl 0-1, Phelps 1-1, Williams 0-1)
Technical Fouls: None
Officials: Scagliotta, Hartzell, Steed

NORTH CAROLINA 82 / CLEMSON 72

SATURDAY, JANUARY 16, 1993
LITTLEJOHN COLISEUM, CLEMSON, S.C.
(ATTENDANCE: 11,000)

North Carolina	FG	FT	REB	A	PF	TP
Reese	3-10	2-6	0	2	1	9
Lynch	7-11	3-6	13	1	2	17
Montross	5-7	3-4	10	2	5	13
Rodl	2-8	4-5	3	3	1	10
Phelps	5-11	1-3	3	2	5	11
Sullivan	1-3	4-6	2	1	2	7
Williams	4-7	3-4	3	0	2	13
Calabria	0-3	0-0	1	0	0	0
Salvadori	0-3	2-2	6	1	2	2
Wenstrom	0-0	0-0	0	0	0	0
Davis	0-0	0-0	0	0	0	0
Cherry	0-0	0-0	0	0	0	0
Totals	27-63	22-36	45	12	20	82

Clemson	FG	FT	REB	A	PF	TP
Gray	7-9	1-2	1	1	5	16
Hines	5-9	2-4	3	0	0	12
Wright	1-4	0-0	5	1	5	2
Richie	0-1	0-0	0	3	4	0
Whitney	5-12	4-4	4	3	3	17
Bovain	4-12	3-4	5	6	5	13
Buckingham	5-8	0-2	9	0	2	10
Martin	0-5	2-2	0	2	1	2
Kelly	0-1	0-0	1	1	0	0
Totals	27-61	12-18	33	17	25	72

North Carolina	31	51 — 82
Clemson	24	48 — 72

Turnovers: UNC 18 (Montross, Phelps, Sullivan 3); Clemson 21 (Whitney 6)
Blocked Shots: UNC 2 (Montross, Salvadori); Clemson 5 (Wright 3)
Steals: UNC 9 (Phelps 3); Clemson 14 (Buckingham 5)
Field Goal Pct.: UNC .429; Clemson .443
Free Throw Pct.: UNC .611; Clemson .667
Three-Point Field Goal Pct.: UNC .250; Clemson .286
Three-Point Field Goal Shooting: UNC (Reese 1-5, Rodl 2-7, Phelps 0-2, Sullivan 1-2, Williams 2-5, Calabria 0-3); Clemson (Gray 1-2, Whitney 3-8, Bovain 2-5, Martin 0-5, Kelly 0-1)
Technical Fouls: Wright
Officials: Wirtz, Rose, Wall

HUGH MORTON

North Carolina governor Jim Hunt, seen with Dean Smith in an early round NCAA game, also was governor in '82 when the Tar Heels won the national title.

NORTH CAROLINA 80 / VIRGINIA 58

WEDNESDAY, JANUARY 20, 1993
SMITH CENTER, CHAPEL HILL, N.C.
(ATTENDANCE: 21,572)

Virginia	FG	FT	REB	A	PF	TP
Parker	2-5	1-2	6	3	2	5
Burrough	5-17	0-0	5	1	2	10
Jeffries	1-3	0-0	4	0	4	2
Williford	2-6	2-2	1	1	3	6
Co. Alexander	4-12	2-2	5	3	2	11
Barnes	2-5	0-1	4	0	2	4
Smith	6-8	0-0	1	1	0	16
Wilson	1-1	0-0	0	0	2	2
Havlicek	0-2	0-2	0	0	0	0
Ch. Alexander	1-1	0-0	2	0	0	2
Totals	**24-60**	**5-9**	**29**	**9**	**17**	**58**

North Carolina	FG	FT	REB	A	PF	TP
Reese	3-6	3-4	3	2	1	10
Lynch	5-12	2-4	11	3	2	12
Montross	5-8	2-3	6	1	3	12
Rodl	4-4	0-0	1	3	0	11
Phelps	2-7	2-2	5	5	3	7
Sullivan	2-5	0-0	2	0	0	5
Williams	1-8	1-1	5	5	1	3
Salvadori	6-10	2-3	5	0	1	14
Calabria	0-0	0-0	0	0	0	0
Wenstrom	1-1	0-0	2	0	0	2
Cherry	0-0	2-2	1	1	0	2
Geth	1-1	0-0	1	0	1	2
Davis	0-1	0-0	0	0	0	0
Stephenson	0-0	0-0	0	0	1	0
Totals	**30-63**	**14-19**	**43**	**20**	**13**	**80**

Virginia	25	33 —	58
North Carolina	32	48 —	80

Turnovers: Virginia 18 (Parker 6); UNC 17 (Reese 4)
Blocked Shots: Virginia 6 (Jeffries, Barnes 2); UNC 4 (Lynch, Montross 2)
Steals: Virginia 5 (Williford 2); UNC 10 (Reese, Lynch 3)
Field Goal Pct.: Virginia .400; UNC .476
Free Throw Pct.: Virginia .556; UNC .737
Three-Point Field Goal Pct.: Virginia .357; UNC .500
Three-Point Field Goal Shooting: Virginia (Williford 0-2, Co. Alexander 1-6, Smith 4-5, Havlicek 0-1); UNC (Reese 1-2, Rodl 3-3, Phelps 1-1, Sullivan 1-2, Williams 0-4)
Technical Fouls: None
Officials: Paparo, Edsall, Donato

NORTH CAROLINA 82 / FLORIDA STATE 77

WEDNESDAY, JANUARY 27, 1993
SMITH CENTER, CHAPEL HILL, N.C.
(ATTENDANCE: 21,572)

Florida State	FG	FT	REB	A	PF	TP
Sura	6-18	2-2	6	1	2	15
Dobard	8-12	1-4	10	2	4	17
Edwards	6-13	3-4	12	5	4	16
Cassell	5-18	2-2	2	4	3	15
Ward	2-4	0-0	6	5	3	5
Wells	0-0	0-0	1	0	0	0
Carroll	0-0	0-0	1	0	0	0
Robinson	4-6	1-1	5	0	0	9
Totals	**31-71**	**9-13**	**45**	**17**	**16**	**77**

North Carolina	FG	FT	REB	A	PF	TP
Sullivan	0-3	0-0	0	1	1	0
Lynch	5-14	3-4	10	3	0	14
Montross	7-10	1-2	8	1	3	15
Rodl	4-9	0-0	5	2	2	11
Cherry	0-0	0-0	2	0	0	0
Phelps	1-8	2-2	3	7	3	4
Reese	2-9	1-2	1	1	1	5
Salvadori	3-4	0-2	5	0	1	6
Williams	5-12	8-8	1	0	2	19
Wenstrom	4-5	0-1	3	0	0	8
Calabria	0-1	0-0	0	0	0	0
Totals	**31-75**	**15-21**	**40**	**15**	**13**	**82**

Florida State	45	32 —	77
North Carolina	28	54 —	82

Turnovers: Florida State 23 (Ward 10); UNC 14 (Phelps 4)
Blocked Shots: Florida State 7 (Dobard 6); UNC 6 (Rodl, Salvadori 2)
Steals: Florida State 12 (Sura, Edwards, Ward 3); UNC 13 (Lynch 7)
Field Goal Pct.: Florida State .437; UNC .413
Free Throw Pct.: Florida State .692; UNC .714
Three-Point Field Goal Pct.: Florida State .240; UNC .250
Three-Point Field Goal Shooting: Florida State (Sura 1-7, Edwards 1-3, Cassell 3-12, Ward 1-3); UNC (Lynch 1-1, Rodl 3-6, Phelps 0-4, Reese 0-3, Williams 1-6)
Technical Fouls: Florida State bench
Officials: Wirtz, Rose, Pitts

WAKE FOREST 88 / NORTH CAROLINA 62

SATURDAY, JANUARY 30, 1993
L. B. JOEL MEMORIAL COLISEUM, WINSTON-SALEM, N.C.
(ATTENDANCE: 14,475)

North Carolina	FG	FT	REB	A	PF	TP
Lynch	5-13	1-1	9	0	3	12
Reese	7-12	0-0	1	2	0	16
Montross	1-5	2-2	1	0	5	4
Phelps	4-4	0-0	4	4	3	8
Rodl	0-4	0-0	1	2	0	0
Sullivan	3-6	0-0	3	1	3	7
Cherry	0-2	2-2	2	1	1	2
Williams	4-9	0-0	1	1	2	9
Salvadori	1-4	0-0	2	0	2	2
Wenstrom	0-2	0-0	2	0	0	0
Stephenson	0-0	0-0	0	0	0	0
Davis	1-3	0-0	2	0	1	2
Totals	**26-64**	**5-5**	**31**	**10**	**22**	**62**

Wake Forest	FG	FT	REB	A	PF	TP
Rogers	6-12	5-7	4	3	3	17
Owens	8-15	0-0	6	2	2	16
Hicks	3-3	9-14	8	0	2	15
Childress	9-13	2-3	5	3	3	27
Harrison	0-3	2-2	2	7	0	2
Banks	1-1	0-0	0	0	0	2
Blucas	2-2	0-1	1	1	0	6
Castle	1-1	0-0	0	0	0	2
LaRue	0-0	0-0	0	0	0	0
Rasmussen	0-0	0-0	0	0	0	0
Fitzgibbons	0-0	0-0	0	0	0	0
King	0-0	1-2	1	0	1	1
Totals	**30-50**	**19-29**	**32**	**16**	**11**	**88**

North Carolina	30	32 —	62
Wake Forest	33	55 —	88

Turnovers: UNC 17 (Phelps 5); Wake 13 (Childress 4)
Blocked Shots: UNC 1 (Lynch); Wake 2 (Hicks, Rasmussen)
Steals: UNC 8 (Phelps 3); Wake Forest 9 (Rogers 4)
Field Goal Pct.: UNC .406; Wake Forest .600
Free Throw Pct.: UNC 1.000; Wake Forest .655
Three-Point Field Goal Pct.: UNC .278; Wake .643
Three-Point Field Goal Shooting: UNC (Lynch 1-2, Reese 2-3, Rodl 0-4, Sullivan 1-2, Cherry 0-1, Williams 1-4, Wenstrom 0-1, Davis 0-1); Wake Forest (Rogers 0-2, Childress 7-9, Harrison 0-1, Blucas 2-2)
Technical Fouls: None
Officials: Moreau, Gray, Gordon

NORTH CAROLINA 70 / SETON HALL 66

SUNDAY, JANUARY 24, 1993
BRENDON BYRNE ARENA, EAST RUTHERFORD, N.J.
(ATTENDANCE: 20,029)

North Carolina	FG	FT	REB	A	PF	TP
Reese	2-6	2-4	3	1	1	6
Lynch	9-15	7-8	7	0	1	25
Montross	3-11	7-10	4	0	4	13
Sullivan	1-3	4-4	2	1	2	6
Phelps	5-7	2-4	3	6	1	12
Rodl	1-1	0-0	1	3	2	2
Cherry	0-0	0-0	0	1	0	0
Williams	1-6	0-0	2	0	0	3
Salvadori	1-2	1-2	1	0	4	3
Wenstrom	0-1	0-0	0	0	0	0
Totals	**23-52**	**23-32**	**26**	**12**	**15**	**70**

Seton Hall	FG	FT	REB	A	PF	TP
Walker	5-6	0-0	7	3	3	10
Karnishovas	5-9	2-2	4	2	4	15
Wright	4-8	3-5	14	0	3	11
Hurley	0-4	0-0	0	2	2	0
Dehere	4-12	2-2	1	2	4	10
Griffin	2-3	1-2	4	0	0	5
Caver	2-5	0-1	3	7	2	4
Leahy	3-4	2-2	1	1	2	11
Shipp	0-1	0-0	1	0	1	0
Totals	**23-52**	**10-14**	**35**	**17**	**21**	**66**

North Carolina	30	40 —	70
Seton Hall	32	34 —	66

Turnovers: UNC 9 (Lynch, Montross, Phelps, Williams 2); Seton Hall 23 (Caver 7)
Blocked Shots: UNC 4 (Salvadori 2); Seton Hall 7 (Wright 4)
Steals: UNC 10 (Phelps 4); Seton Hall 5 (Wright 3)
Field Goal Pct.: UNC .442; Seton Hall .481
Free Throw Pct.: UNC .719; Seton Hall .714
Three-Point Field Goal Pct.: UNC .200; Seton Hall .462
Three-Point Field Goal Shooting: UNC (Reese 0-1, Phelps 0-1, Williams 1-3); Seton Hall (Karnishovas 3-3, Dehere 0-4, Caver 0-2, Leahy 3-4)
Technical Fouls: UNC bench
Officials: Higgins, Gray, Scagliotta

HUGH MORTON

Junior Kevin Salvadori led the Tar Heels with 14 points as UNC handed Virginia its first loss of the season.

DUKE 81 / NORTH CAROLINA 67

WEDNESDAY, FEBRUARY 3, 1993
CAMERON INDOOR STADIUM, DURHAM, N.C.
(ATTENDANCE: 9,314)

North Carolina	FG	FT	REB	A	PF	TP
Reese	3-6	0-0	2	0	3	6
Lynch	7-15	3-4	8	3	5	17
Montross	8-15	6-11	13	0	4	22
Rodl	1-2	0-1	1	4	1	2
Phelps	1-5	1-2	3	2	4	4
Sullivan	2-5	5-5	3	1	2	9
Williams	3-15	0-1	4	2	4	7
Salvadori	0-1	0-0	2	0	4	0
Wenstrom	0-1	0-0	0	0	0	0
Calabria	0-1	0-0	1	0	2	0
Totals	25-66	15-24	40	12	29	67

Duke	FG	FT	REB	A	PF	TP
G. Hill	5-12	5-6	8	3	3	15
Clark	1-3	0-0	4	2	1	2
Parks	6-7	2-3	9	0	4	14
Hurley	4-12	8-8	4	7	3	20
T. Hill	6-12	4-7	4	2	1	16
Lang	3-6	4-4	5	1	4	10
Blakeney	0-1	0-0	0	0	1	0
Meek	1-1	2-3	0	1	0	4
Collins	0-2	0-0	0	1	1	0
Brown	0-0	0-0	0	0	0	0
Totals	26-56	25-31	36	17	18	81

North Carolina	32	35	— 67
Duke	34	47	— 81

Turnovers: UNC 15 (Reese 4); Duke 12 (Clark, Hurley, Lang 3)
Blocked Shots: UNC 0; Duke 5 (Parks 4)
Steals: UNC 5 (Montross, Rodl 2); Duke 7 (Hurley 3)
Field Goal Pct.: UNC .379; Duke 464
Free Throw Pct.: UNC .625; Duke .806
Three-Point Field Goal Pct.: UNC .133; Duke .267
Three-Point Field Goal Shooting: UNC (Reese 0-1, Lynch 0-2, Rodl 0-1, Phelps 1-1, Sullivan 0-1, Williams 1-8, Calabria 0-1); Duke (Clark 0-2, Hurley 4-8. T. Hill 0-3, Collins 0-2)
Technical Fouls: None
Officials: Scagliotta, Hartzell, Donato

NORTH CAROLINA 104 / N.C. STATE 58

SATURDAY, FEBRUARY 6, 1993
SMITH CENTER, CHAPEL HILL, N.C.
(ATTENDANCE: 21,572)

N. C. State	FG	FT	REB	A	PF	TP
Davis	3-8	1-2	6	1	1	8
Lewis	6-13	1-3	7	0	3	13
Thompson	7-9	1-2	14	2	3	15
McCuller	2-10	1-2	3	5	2	5
Marshall	1-4	0-0	1	0	1	2
Fuller	4-8	0-0	3	1	5	8
Wilson	1-5	2-2	1	0	3	4
Newman	1-5	0-1	0	1	2	3
Totals	25-62	6-12	36	10	20	58

North Carolina	FG	FT	REB	A	PF	TP
Sullivan	6-13	0-0	3	2	1	12
Lynch	6-10	2-5	5	5	1	14
Montross	6-10	1-1	8	1	2	13
Rodl	4-8	4-4	5	4	3	12
Phelps	4-9	0-1	4	9	0	10
Williams	5-9	0-0	1	0	0	12
Salvadori	2-4	2-4	4	0	1	6
Wenstrom	1-5	1-2	5	0	2	3
Calabria	1-2	0-1	1	2	2	3
Cherry	2-2	0-0	2	3	1	5
Davis	1-3	6-7	4	0	0	8
Geth	2-2	2-2	3	0	0	6
Stephenson	0-0	0-0	0	2	0	0
Totals	40-77	18-27	45	28	13	104

N. C. State	23	35	— 58
North Carolina	43	61	—104

Turnovers: N.C. State 30 (Lewis 6); UNC 16 (Rodl, Phelps, Cherry 3)
Blocked Shots: N.C. State 1 (Thompson); UNC 6 (Salvadori 2)
Steals: N.C. State 5 (5 with 1 each); UNC 19 (Lynch, Rodl, Phelps, Williams 3)
Field Goal Pct.: N.C. State .403; UNC .519
Free Throw Pct.: N.C. State .500; UNC .667
Three-Point Field Goal Pct.: N.C. State .133; UNC .333
Three-Point Field Goal Shooting: N. C. State (Davis 1-3, McCuller 0-4, Marshall 0-1, Wilson 0-2, Newman 1-5); UNC (Sullivan 0-3, Rodl 0-3, Phelps 2-2, Williams 2-6, Calabria 1-1, Cherry 1-1, Davis 0-2);
Technical Fouls: None
Officials: Wirtz, Rose, Wood

NORTH CAROLINA 77 / MARYLAND 63

TUESDAY, FEBRUARY 9, 1993
COLE FIELD HOUSE, COLLEGE PARK, MD.
(ATTENDANCE: 14,500)

North Carolina	FG	FT	REB	A	PF	TP
Sullivan	4-6	2-4	2	0	3	10
Lynch	4-10	4-4	12	1	3	12
Montross	7-8	3-5	7	0	3	17
Rodl	0-3	2-2	1	6	1	2
Phelps	5-8	0-0	8	2	2	11
Williams	2-9	5-5	5	2	0	9
Reese	3-7	0-0	1	2	1	6
Salvadori	2-5	0-1	6	0	2	4
Calabria	1-1	2-2	0	1	0	5
Wenstrom	0-0	0-0	0	0	0	0
Cherry	0-0	1-2	0	0	0	1
Totals	28-57	19-25	44	14	15	77

Maryland	FG	FT	REB	A	PF	TP
Hipp	7-13	0-0	6	4	4	16
Burns	3-13	4-4	4	1	3	10
Kerwin	1-5	2-2	2	0	3	4
Rhodes	5-12	0-0	4	4	5	13
McLinton	0-7	4-4	7	6	2	4
Lucas	4-6	1-2	3	1	3	10
Simpkins	1-2	0-1	0	1	1	2
Shultz	0-0	0-0	0	0	0	0
Bristol	1-4	2-2	3	1	0	4
Walsh	0-0	0-0	0	0	0	0
Totals	22-62	13-15	30	18	21	63

North Carolina	30	47	— 77
Maryland	23	40	— 63

Turnovers: UNC 22 (Lynch 7); Maryland 20 (Rhodes 6)
Blocked Shots: UNC 4 (Lynch 2); Maryland 4 (Hipp, Burns, Rhodes, McLinton 1)
Steals: UNC 6 (Phelps, Williams 2); Maryland 6 (Hipp 3)
Field Goal Pct.: UNC .491; Maryland .355
Free Throw Pct.: UNC .760; Maryland .867
Three-Point Field Goal Pct.: UNC .286; Maryland .400
Three-Point Field Goal Shooting: UNC (Rodl 0-2, Phelps 1-2, Williams 0-1, Reese 0-1, Calabria 1-1); Maryland (Hipp 2-3, Rhodes 3-9, Lucas 1-1, Bristol 0-2)
Technical Fouls: None
Officials: Paparo, Edsall, Styons

HUGH MORTON

With shots like this, it didn't take Eric Montross and the Tar Heels long to put away N.C. State for the second time of the season. Six players scored in double figures for UNC that day.

NORTH CAROLINA 77
GEORGIA TECH 66

SUNDAY, FEBRUARY 14, 1993
ALEXANDER MEMORIAL COLISEUM, ATLANTA, GA.
(ATTENDANCE: 9,922)

North Carolina	FG	FT	REB	A	PF	TP
Rodl	1-2	0-0	1	5	1	3
Lynch	3-8	1-2	4	0	5	7
Montross	4-8	4-5	9	1	3	12
Phelps	5-8	2-2	2	7	1	13
Reese	4-9	0-0	3	1	1	9
Sullivan	0-4	4-6	4	1	4	4
Williams	8-15	2-4	1	2	3	21
Salvadori	4-7	0-0	6	1	0	8
Wenstrom	0-0	0-0	1	0	0	0
Calabria	0-0	0	0	0	0	0
Cherry	0-0	0-0	0	0	1	0
Totals	29-61	13-19	34	18	19	77

Georgia Tech	FG	FT	REB	A	PF	TP
Moore	2-9	0-0	6	2	3	4
Forrest	7-12	4-5	13	1	3	18
Mackey	2-7	3-3	5	0	3	7
Best	6-12	3-3	2	1	3	17
Barry	4-7	2-2	3	6	2	13
Hill	1-4	3-4	1	3	4	5
Newbill	1-2	0-0	1	0	0	2
Balanis	0-0	0-0	0	0	0	0
Harlicka	0-0	0-0	0	0	0	0
Totals	23-53	15-17	33	13	18	66

North Carolina	31	46 —	77
Georgia Tech	36	30 —	66

Turnovers: UNC 11 (Williams 3); Georgia Tech 18 (Mackey, Barry 5)
Blocked Shots: UNC 3 (Montross, Williams, Salvadori); Georgia Tech 3 (Forrest 2)
Steals: UNC 12 (Phelps 4); Georgia Tech 4 (Forrest, Mackey, Best, Hill 1)
Field Goal Pct.: UNC .475; Georgia Tech .434
Free Throw Pct.: UNC .684; Georgia Tech .882
Three-Point Field Goal Pct.: UNC .462; Georgia Tech .385
Three-Point Field Goal Shooting: UNC (Rodl 1-2, Phelps 1-1, Reese 1-2, Sullivan 0-1, Williams 3-7); Georgia Tech (Moore 0-3, Best 2-3, Barry 3-4, Hill 0-2, Newbill 0-1)
Technical Fouls: Georgia Tech bench
Officials: Wirtz, Rose, Gordon

NORTH CAROLINA 80
CLEMSON 67

WEDNESDAY, FEBRUARY 17, 1993
SMITH CENTER, CHAPEL HILL, N.C.
(ATTENDANCE: 21,147)

Clemson	FG	FT	REB	A	PF	TP
Brown	4-13	0-0	0	4	3	10
Buckingham	1-3	0-0	1	1	3	2
Wright	8-12	4-6	12	0	4	20
Whitney	8-11	0-0	4	6	2	24
Bovain	1-1	0-0	1	0	0	2
Gray	2-8	3-4	5	0	2	7
Martin	0-3	0-0	2	0	0	0
Tomera	0-1	0-0	0	0	2	0
Richie	1-1	0-0	2	3	2	2
Totals	25-53	7-10	29	14	18	67

North Carolina	FG	FT	REB	A	PF	TP
Reese	8-11	0-0	4	1	1	18
Lynch	4-11	0-0	5	2	1	8
Montross	9-15	4-6	7	1	3	22
Rodl	1-2	0-0	2	6	1	2
Phelps	6-12	0-0	6	8	0	12
Calabria	2-3	0-0	0	0	0	4
Sullivan	1-1	0-0	0	1	0	3
Williams	1-4	6-8	1	2	2	8
Salvadori	1-1	0-0	2	0	0	2
Wenstrom	0-0	1-2	1	0	0	1
Cherry	0-0	0-0	0	0	0	0
Davis	0-0	0-0	0	0	0	0
Geth	0-0	0-0	0	0	0	0
Totals	33-60	11-16	29	21	8	80

Clemson	26	41 —	67
North Carolina	36	44 —	80

Turnovers: Clemson 22 (Whitney, Richie 4); UNC 14 (Phelps 5)
Blocked Shots: Clemson 7 (Wright 7); UNC 4 (Montross 4)
Steals: Clemson 11 (Whitney 5); UNC 16 (Lynch 5)
Field Goal Pct.: Clemson .471; UNC .550
Free Throw Pct.: Clemson .700; UNC .688
Three-Point Field Goal Pct.: Clemson .526; UNC .300
Three-Point Field Goal Shooting: Clemson (Brown 2-5, Whitney 8-10, Gray 0-1, Martin 0-3); UNC (Reese 2-3, Rodl 0-1, Phelps 0-2, Calabria 0-1, Sullivan 1-1, Williams 0-2)
Technical Fouls: None
Officials: Scagliotta, Lembo, Pitts

NORTH CAROLINA 78
VIRGINIA 58

SUNDAY, FEBRUARY 21, 1993
UNIVERSITY HALL, CHARLOTTESVILLE, VA.
(ATTENDANCE: 8,864)

North Carolina	FG	FT	REB	A	PF	TP
Reese	4-8	2-4	6	2	0	11
Lynch	6-11	5-5	11	3	2	17
Montross	7-13	3-4	7	1	5	17
Phelps	3-8	3-3	7	5	2	10
Williams	1-4	0-0	2	1	3	2
Rodl	0-1	4-4	2	2	0	4
Sullivan	3-3	4-4	0	0	1	10
Salvadori	0-2	0-0	1	0	3	0
Wenstrom	1-3	0-0	1	0	2	2
Calabria	1-2	0-0	0	2	1	2
Cherry	0-0	1-2	0	0	0	1
Geth	0-1	0-0	1	0	0	0
Davis	1-1	0-0	0	0	0	2
Stephenson	0-0	0-0	0	0	0	0
Totals	27-57	22-26	40	16	18	78

Virginia	FG	FT	REB	A	PF	TP
Burrough	7-15	5-6	9	0	1	19
Williford	1-1	0-0	0	1	3	2
Jeffries	2-8	4-4	6	0	4	8
Parker	1-11	1-2	5	2	3	4
Co. Alexander	4-14	0-1	3	6	2	10
Smith	2-7	2-2	3	2	3	8
Barnes	1-2	0-0	5	0	2	2
Havlicek	0-3	0-0	2	1	1	0
Wilson	2-3	1-2	4	0	2	5
Ch. Alexander	0-0	0-0	1	0	0	0
Graves	0-0	0-0	0	0	0	0
Totals	20-64	13-17	39	12	21	58

North Carolina	42	36 —	78
Virginia	22	36 —	58

Turnovers: UNC 12 (Phelps 4); Virginia 16 (Co. Alexander 5)
Blocked Shots: UNC 1 (Wenstrom); Virginia 4 (Jeffries 2)
Steals: UNC 5 (Lynch, Phelps, Sullivan, Cherry, Davis 1); Virginia 6 (Co. Alexander 2)
Field Goal Pct.: UNC .474; Virginia .313
Free Throw Pct.: UNC .846; Virginia .765
Three-Point Field Goal Pct.: UNC .250; Virginia .278
Three-Point Field Goal Shooting: UNC (Reese 1-2, Phelps 1-2, Williams 0-2, Rodl 0-1, Calabria 0-1); Virginia (Parker 1-5, Co. Alexander 2-6, Smith 2-7)
Technical Fouls: None
Officials: Paparo, Edsall, Wood

North Carolina's starters got a rare early breather as the Tar Heels raced to a 45-point NCAA win over Rhode Island.

NORTH CAROLINA 85
NOTRE DAME 56

TUESDAY, FEBRUARY 23, 1993
SMITH CENTER, CHAPEL HILL, N.C.
(ATTENDANCE: 21,572)

Notre Dame	FG	FT	REB	A	PF	TP
Bi. Taylor	2-6	1-2	1	0	3	5
Williams	8-21	4-4	5	1	1	20
Jon Ross	2-4	0-0	5	1	3	4
Justice	1-4	0-0	1	3	2	3
Hoover	4-11	2-2	2	2	4	12
Boyer	0-2	0-0	1	1	4	0
Russell	1-1	2-4	3	1	2	4
Joe Ross	2-3	0-0	2	2	5	4
Ryan	0-0	1-2	0	0	0	1
Adamson	1-3	0-0	1	0	0	3
Keaney	0-0	0-0	0	0	0	0
Totals	**21-55**	**10-14**	**24**	**11**	**24**	**56**

North Carolina	FG	FT	REB	A	PF	TP
Reese	3-7	5-6	8	4	0	11
Lynch	3-7	0-0	8	2	2	6
Montross	6-9	7-11	4	0	2	19
Williams	3-8	0-0	3	1	2	7
Phelps	1-3	4-8	3	4	1	6
Sullivan	3-6	1-1	0	2	0	7
Rodl	1-2	0-0	0	1	1	2
Salvadori	3-6	2-2	6	0	2	8
Wenstrom	2-3	0-0	4	0	2	4
Calabria	0-1	0-0	2	1	1	0
Cherry	2-4	2-3	3	1	1	6
Davis	1-3	0-2	1	0	0	2
Geth	1-1	1-2	2	0	3	3
Stephenson	2-2	0-0	1	0	0	4
Landry	0-1	0-0	1	1	1	0
Totals	**31-63**	**22-35**	**47**	**17**	**18**	**85**

Notre Dame	27	29 —	56
North Carolina	40	45 —	85

Turnovers: Notre Dame 19 (Williams 4); UNC 13 (Montross, Cherry 3)
Blocked Shots: Notre Dame 1 (Hoover); UNC 4 (Lynch, Salvadori 2)
Steals: Notre Dame 6 (Joe Ross 4); UNC 12 (Lynch, Phelps 3)
Field Goal Pct.: Notre Dame .382; UNC .492
Free Throw Pct.: Notre Dame .714; UNC .629
Three-Point Field Goal Pct.: Notre Dame .250; UNC .091
Three-Point Field Goal Shooting: Notre Dame (Williams 0-3, Jon Ross 0-1, Justice 1-1, Hoover 2-8, Boyer 0-1, Adamson 1-2); UNC (Reese 0-1, Williams 1-5, Phelps 0-1, Sullivan 0-1, Rodl 0-1, Calabria 0-1, Davis 0-1)
Technical Fouls: None
Officials: Parramore, Rodeneffer, Clark

NORTH CAROLINA 86
FLORIDA STATE 76

SATURDAY, FEBRUARY 27, 1993
TALLAHASSEE-LEON CO. CIVIC CENTER, TALLAHASSEE, FLA.
(ATTENDANCE: 13,251)

North Carolina	FG	FT	REB	A	PF	TP
Montross	5-10	5-5	5	1	3	15
Phelps	2-2	0-2	6	10	1	4
Williams	3-12	6-6	1	0	2	13
Reese	11-18	2-3	6	1	0	25
Lynch	7-14	2-2	10	1	4	16
Sullivan	0-2	2-2	3	1	3	2
Rodl	2-2	0-2	0	2	2	6
Calabria	1-1	1-2	2	1	0	3
Salvadori	1-4	0-0	3	0	2	2
Totals	**32-65**	**18-24**	**40**	**17**	**17**	**86**

Florida State	FG	FT	REB	A	PF	TP
Cassell	5-11	6-7	4	5	4	18
Sura	6-17	1-3	3	5	2	14
Edwards	9-13	5-6	10	4	1	23
Wells	3-8	0-0	5	1	4	6
Dobard	4-6	1-2	3	0	5	9
Hands	0-1	0	0	0	0	0
Robinson	3-6	0-1	3	0	3	6
Totals	**30-62**	**13-19**	**31**	**15**	**19**	**76**

North Carolina	33	53 —	86
Florida State	33	43 —	76

Turnovers: UNC 15 (Phelps 6); Florida State 18 (Cassell 6)
Blocked Shots: UNC 4 (Salvadori 2); Florida State 6 (Edwards 4)
Steals: UNC 11 (Lynch 5); Florida State 9 (Cassell 5)
Field Goal Pct.: UNC .492; Florida State .484
Free Throw Pct.: UNC .750; Florida State .684
Three-Point Field Goal Pct.: UNC .364; Florida State .143
Three-Point Field Goal Shooting: UNC (Williams 1-6, Reese 1-3, Rodl 2-2); Florida State (Cassell 2-5, Sura 1-12, Edwards 0-1, Wells 0-3)
Technical Fouls: Montross, Sura, Salvadori
Officials: Herring, Croft, Rote

NORTH CAROLINA 83
WAKE FOREST 65

WEDNESDAY, MARCH 3, 1993
SMITH CENTER, CHAPEL HILL, N.C.
(ATTENDANCE: 21,572)

Wake Forest	FG	FT	REB	A	PF	TP
Owens	3-11	0-0	3	2	1	6
Rogers	4-12	4-6	8	3	5	12
Hicks	3-3	0-0	5	3	2	6
Childress	5-10	2-2	1	4	5	16
Harrison	2-4	0-0	0	4	0	4
Blucas	4-7	2-2	2	1	2	14
Banks	1-1	1-1	0	0	0	3
Rasmussen	1-2	0-0	3	0	2	3
Castle	0-0	1-2	0	0	0	1
LaRue	0-1	0-0	0	0	0	0
Fitzgibbons	0-0	0-0	0	0	0	0
Canty	0-0	0-0	0	0	0	0
Totals	**23-51**	**10-13**	**22**	**17**	**17**	**65**

North Carolina	FG	FT	REB	A	PF	TP
Reese	6-11	1-2	3	4	0	16
Lynch	9-16	0-0	7	4	0	18
Montross	7-8	3-4	6	0	3	17
Williams	4-9	3-4	1	0	1	13
Phelps	2-5	0-0	5	7	4	4
Sullivan	1-3	0-0	0	1	1	2
Rodl	2-4	0-0	2	2	1	4
Salvadori	1-2	5-6	7	0	2	7
Calabria	0-1	0-0	1	0	1	0
Davis	0-0	0-0	0	0	0	0
Cherry	0-0	0-0	0	0	0	0
Geth	0-0	0-0	0	0	1	0
Wenstrom	1-1	0-0	0	0	0	2
Totals	**33-60**	**12-16**	**33**	**19**	**14**	**83**

Wake Forest	27	38 —	65
North Carolina	45	38 —	83

Turnovers: Wake Forest 15 (Childress 4); UNC 9 (Lynch 3)
Blocked Shots: Wake Forest 3 (Hicks 3); UNC 2 (Montross 2)
Steals: Wake Forest 3 (Rogers 2); UNC 6 (Lynch 2)
Field Goal Pct.: Wake Forest .451; UNC .550
Free Throw Pct.: Wake Forest .769; UNC .750
Three-Point Field Goal Pct.: Wake Forest .500; UNC .556
Three-Point Field Goal Shooting: Wake Forest (Owens 0-1, Rogers 0-2, Childress 4-6, Blucas 4-6, Rasmussen 1-2, LaRue 0-1); UNC (Reese 3-3, Williams 2-3, Phelps 0-1, Rodl 0-1, Calabria 0-1)
Technical Fouls: None
Officials: Paparo, Edsall, Greenwood

HUGH MORTON

Former ACC official Hank Nichols (L), who now works for the NCAA, played a part in Carolina history. He officiated in both Final Four games in 1982 in New Orleans when Dean Smith and the Tar Heels beat Houston and Georgetown.

NORTH CAROLINA 83 — DUKE 69

SUNDAY, MARCH 7, 1993
SMITH CENTER, CHAPEL HILL, N.C. (ATTENDANCE: 21,572)

Duke	FG	FT	REB	A	PF	TP
T. Hill	4-13	4-4	2	1	4	13
Lang	1-6	3-4	9	0	3	5
Parks	3-6	1-1	2	0	2	7
Collins	4-10	3-4	4	5	1	15
Hurley	2-12	1-3	4	6	1	6
Clark	4-6	1-2	2	2	4	12
Blakeney	2-4	1-1	2	1	0	5
Meek	2-4	1-1	3	1	2	4
Brown	0-0	2-3	2	0	0	2
Brunson	0-1	0-0	1	0	0	0
Totals	22-62	16-22	31	16	17	69

North Carolina	FG	FT	REB	A	PF	TP
Lynch	6-10	0-3	11	1	4	12
Stephenson	1-1	0-0	0	0	0	2
Wenstrom	0-0	0-0	1	0	0	0
Rodl	0-1	0-2	0	3	0	0
Cherry	1-2	0-0	0	0	0	2
Phelps	3-6	2-2	9	7	2	8
Montross	6-9	6-11	7	1	3	18
Williams	10-15	2-2	1	1	3	27
Reese	4-8	2-4	4	3	1	10
Sullivan	1-3	0-0	2	0	2	2
Salvadori	1-3	0-0	3	1	1	2
Davis	0-1	0-0	0	0	1	0
Calabria	0-0	0-0	0	1	0	0
Geth	0-1	0-0	1	0	1	0
Totals	33-60	12-24	43	18	18	83

Duke	30	39	—	69
North Carolina	40	43	—	83

Turnovers: Duke 13 (T. Hill 4); UNC 15 (Phelps 5)
Blocked Shots: Duke 4 (Lang 2); UNC 9 (Montross 3)
Steals: Duke 10 (Hurley 3); UNC 5 (Sullivan 2)
Field Goal Pct.: Duke .355; UNC .550
Free Throw Pct.: Duke .727; UNC .500
Three-Point Field Goal Pct.: Duke .346; UNC .417
Three-Point Field Goal Shooting: Duke (T. Hill 1-5, Lang 0-1, Collins 4-8, Hurley 1-7, Clark 3-3, Blakeney 0-2); UNC (Phelps 0-2, Williams 5-8, Reese 0-2)
Technical Fouls: Hurley
Officials: Wirtz, Rose, Gordon

NORTH CAROLINA 102 — MARYLAND 66

FRIDAY, MARCH 12, 1993
CHARLOTTE COLISEUM, CHARLOTTE, N.C.
(ATTENDANCE: 23,532)
QUARTERFINAL, ACC TOURNAMENT

Maryland	FG	FT	REB	A	PF	TP
Hipp	7-15	3-4	0	2	2	19
Burns	6-18	2-6	11	2	5	14
Kerwin	0-2	0-0	2	1	3	0
Rhodes	6-12	0-1	5	3	0	15
McLinton	2-9	0-0	6	3	1	4
Simpkins	3-8	1-2	1	6	3	8
Lucas	1-3	1-2	2	1	4	3
Walsh	0-1	0-0	1	0	1	0
Shultz	0-0	0-0	0	0	1	0
Bristol	1-4	1-2	3	0	0	3
Thibeault	0-1	0-0	0	0	0	0
Totals	26-73	8-17	33	18	20	66

North Carolina	FG	FT	REB	A	PF	TP
Sullivan	3-3	1-1	2	1	2	7
Lynch	9-15	4-5	15	1	1	22
Salvadori	2-5	2-2	5	0	2	6
Phelps	1-5	0-0	3	4	4	2
Williams	2-7	2-2	1	3	0	7
Montross	4-6	3-3	8	0	2	11
Reese	5-11	6-7	6	3	2	16
Rodl	1-3	2-2	1	7	1	4
Calabria	1-6	0-0	3	3	2	2
Cherry	1-1	2-2	0	1	0	5
Wenstrom	2-2	2-2	1	1	0	6
Geth	3-4	1-1	5	0	0	7
Davis	3-6	1-2	2	0	1	7
Stephenson	0-1	0-0	0	0	0	0
Totals	37-75	26-29	57	24	17	102

Maryland	34	32	—	66
North Carolina	51	51	—	102

Turnovers: Maryland 18 (McLinton 5); UNC 17 (Montross 4)
Blocked Shots: Maryland 4 (Burns, Kerwin 2); UNC 3 (Salvadori, Reese, Cherry 1)
Steals: Maryland 9 (Rhodes, McLinton, Simpkins, Lucas 2); UNC 10 (Lynch 3)
Field Goal Pct.: Maryland .356; UNC .493
Free Throw Pct.: Maryland .471; UNC .897
Three-Point Field Goal Pct.: Maryland .316; UNC .250
Three-Point Field Goal Shooting: Maryland (Hipp 2-5, Rhodes 3-7, Simpkins 1-3, Walsh 0-1, Bristol 0-3); UNC (Williams 1-4, Reese 0-1, Rodl 0-1, Calabria 0-1, Cherry 1-1,)
Technical Fouls: None
Officials: Scagliotta, Hartzell, Rote

NORTH CAROLINA 74 — VIRGINIA 56

SATURDAY, MARCH 13, 1993
CHARLOTTE COLISEUM, CHARLOTTE, N.C.
(ATTENDANCE: 23,532)
SEMIFINAL, ACC TOURNAMENT

Virginia	FG	FT	REB	A	PF	TP
Burrough	4-12	1-2	4	1	3	9
Williford	2-6	0-0	4	0	4	4
Jeffries	4-8	0-2	3	1	4	8
Parker	3-6	0-0	7	3	4	7
Co. Alexander	9-18	1-3	1	2	4	22
Smith	2-6	0-0	3	2	1	6
Barnes	0-1	0-0	3	0	0	0
Wilson	0-0	0-0	2	0	1	0
havlicek	0-0	0-0	0	0	0	0
Mitchell	0-1	0-0	0	0	0	0
Totals	24-58	2-7	30	10	21	56

North Carolina	FG	FT	REB	A	PF	TP
Reese	5-10	6-8	5	2	1	16
Lynch	1-11	2-2	11	3	1	4
Montross	3-5	8-8	7	0	3	14
Phelps	3-7	2-2	3	3	1	8
Williams	5-13	6-8	3	0	4	19
Sullivan	4-6	3-4	5	0	1	11
Salvadori	0-3	0-0	3	0	2	0
Cherry	1-1	0-0	1	0	0	2
Rodl	0-0	0-0	1	0	0	0
Calabria	0-1	0-0	0	0	0	0
Geth	0-1	0-0	1	0	0	0
Davis	0-0	0-0	1	0	0	0
Wenstrom	0-0	0-0	0	0	0	0
Stephenson	0-0	0-0	0	0	0	0
Totals	22-58	27-32	43	8	9	74

Virginia	30	26 —	56
North Carolina	35	39 —	74

Turnovers: Virginia 17 (Parker 5); UNC 12 (Montross, Phelps 3)
Blocked Shots: Virginia 0, UNC 4 (Sullivan 2)
Steals: Virginia 9 (Parker 3); UNC 12 (Phelps 3)
Field Goal Pct.: Virginia .414; UNC .379
Free Throw Pct.: Virginia .286; UNC .844
Three-Point Field Goal Pct.: Virginia .316; UNC .375
Three-Point Field Goal Shooting: Virginia (Williford 0-1, Parker 1-3, Co. Alexander 2-6, Mitchell 0-1); UNC (Reese 0-1, Williams 3-6, Sullivan 0-1)
Technical Fouls: None
Officials: Moreau, Rose, Croft

HUGH MORTON

Carolina ended the ACC regular season with a sweet victory over archrival Duke in Chapel Hill. Travis Stephenson hit a jumper at the buzzer that the scoreboard has yet to record for the final 83-69 score.

GEORGIA TECH 77
NORTH CAROLINA 75

SUNDAY, MARCH 14, 1993
CHARLOTTE COLISEUM, CHARLOTTE, N.C.
(ATTENDANCE: 23,532)
FINAL, ATLANTIC COAST CONFERENCE TOURNAMENT

Georgia Tech	FG	FT	REB	A	PF	TP
Moore	2-7	4-4	3	1	2	10
Forrest	11-19	5-6	10	0	3	27
Mackey	2-5	0-1	6	1	4	4
Best	3-14	8-9	3	6	1	14
Barry	4-9	2-2	9	6	0	11
Hill	2-5	2-2	1	2	3	7
Newbill	1-1	2-2	5	0	3	4
Totals	25-60	23-26	39	16	16	77

North Carolina	FG	FT	REB	A	PF	TP
Reese	8-18	6-7	6	0	1	24
Lynch	4-12	0-1	9	2	5	8
Montross	6-11	7-9	17	1	2	19
Rodl	1-1	0-2	0	6	3	2
Williams	4-18	0-0	2	1	4	11
Sullivan	3-5	0-0	3	2	2	7
Cherry	0-2	0-0	1	2	1	0
Salvadori	2-4	0-0	1	0	1	4
Calabria	0-0	0-0	0	0	0	0
Totals	28-71	13-19	43	14	19	75

Georgia Tech	41	36	—	77
North Carolina	37	38	—	75

Turnovers: Georgia Tech 14 (Barry 4); UNC 15 (Lynch 4)
Blocked Shots: Georgia Tech 4 (Forrest, Barry, Hill, Newbill 1); UNC 3 (Montross 2)
Steals: Georgia Tech 4 (Moore 2); UNC 8 (Rodl 3)
Field Goal Pct.: Georgia Tech .417; UNC .394
Free Throw Pct.: Georgia Tech .885; UNC .684
Three-Point Field Goal Pct.: Georgia Tech .250; UNC .286
Three-Point Field Goal Shooting: Georgia Tech (Moore 2-3, Best 0-7, Barry 1-4, Hill 1-2); UNC (Reese 2-5, Lynch 0-1, Williams 3-12, Sullivan 1-2, Cherry 0-1)
Technical Fouls: None
Officials: Wirtz, Paparo, Scagliotta

NORTH CAROLINA 85
EAST CAROLINA 65

THURSDAY, MARCH 18, 1993
JOEL COLISEUM, WINSTON-SALEM, N.C.
(ATTENDANCE: 14,366)
FIRST ROUND, NCAA EAST REGIONAL

East Carolina	FG	FT	REB	A	PF	TP
Young	5-13	0-0	4	1	2	10
Gill	3-10	0-1	5	1	2	6
Copeland	0-2	1-2	7	2	4	1
Lyons	8-11	6-6	4	2	4	27
Richardson	4-9	0-0	1	3	4	10
Peterson	2-5	0-0	2	1	1	6
Lewis	1-3	2-4	5	0	2	4
Hunter	0-3	1-2	1	0	1	1
Totals	23-56	10-15	31	12	20	65

North Carolina	FG	FT	REB	A	PF	TP
Reese	3-7	5-6	2	5	1	11
Lynch	7-9	1-2	8	2	0	15
Montross	6-9	5-7	9	2	2	17
Williams	3-9	0-0	2	0	0	9
Rodl	3-5	3-3	0	4	2	10
Sullivan	0-0	4-4	1	1	0	4
Calabria	0-1	0-0	0	1	2	0
Salvadori	2-4	4-4	4	0	1	8
Phelps	3-6	0-1	2	0	1	6
Davis	1-1	0-0	0	0	0	3
Cherry	1-1	0-0	0	0	0	3
Stephenson	0-0	0-0	0	0	0	0
Wenstrom	0-1	0-0	1	0	0	0
Totals	29-53	22-27	34	15	9	85

East Carolina	34	31	—	65
North Carolina	45	40	—	85

Turnovers: East Carolina 11 (Richardson 4); UNC 8 (Reese 4)
Blocked Shots: East Carolina 1 (Lyons); UNC 4 (Montross 2)
Steals: East Carolina 5 (Copeland 2); UNC 7 (Montross, Phelps 2)
Field Goal Pct.: East Carolina .411; UNC .547
Free Throw Pct.: East Carolina .667; UNC .815
Three-Point Field Goal Pct.: East Carolina .429; UNC .313
Three-Point Field Goal Shooting: East Carolina (Young 0-4, Gill 0-2, Lyons 5-6, Richardson 2-4, Peterson 2-4, Hunter 0-1); UNC (Reese 0-2, Williams 3-9, Rodl 1-2, Calabria 0-1, Phelps 0-1, Davis 1-1)
Technical Fouls: None
Officials: Libby, Day, Shaw

NORTH CAROLINA 112
RHODE ISLAND 67

SATURDAY, MARCH 20, 1993
JOEL COLISEUM, WINSTON-SALEM, N.C.
(ATTENDANCE: 14,366)
SECOND ROUND, NCAA EAST REGIONAL

Rhode Island	FG	FT	REB	A	PF	TP
Brown	5-18	1-2	6	2	1	15
Samuel	7-16	3-4	8	0	1	17
Solis	1-5	3-8	5	0	5	5
Cofield	1-10	0-0	0	3	2	3
Easterling	1-1	2-2	1	1	2	5
Collins	0-0	1-2	1	1	0	1
Fox	5-11	0-0	1	0	4	10
Ivey-Jones	3-6	0-0	3	1	5	7
Keebler	0-1	0-0	2	0	0	0
Cowie	0-0	0-0	1	0	1	0
Moten	0-4	4-4	4	0	5	4
Totals	23-72	14-22	34	8	26	67

North Carolina	FG	FT	REB	A	PF	TP
Reese	3-8	0-0	4	6	2	7
Lynch	4-7	1-2	7	1	1	9
Montross	5-7	5-5	9	2	2	15
Williams	7-11	0-0	2	0	0	17
Phelps	7-7	0-1	2	2	3	15
Sullivan	2-4	5-6	5	5	1	9
Rodl	2-2	0-0	1	5	0	4
Salvadori	4-7	3-5	5	1	3	11
Calabria	0-2	0-0	1	1	0	0
Davis	1-8	1-2	2	1	0	3
Cherry	1-2	3-4	1	3	1	6
Stephenson	0-1	0-0	1	0	0	0
Wenstrom	5-7	4-5	3	1	2	14
Geth	1-1	0-0	0	0	0	2
Totals	42-74	22-30	50	28	15	112

Rhode Island	21	46	—	67
North Carolina	50	62	—	112

Turnovers: Rhode Island 15 (Fox 4); UNC 11 (Rodl, Wenstrom 2)
Blocked Shots: Rhode Island 3 (Samuel, Collins, Fox 1); UNC 6 (Montross 3)
Steals: Rhode Island 8 (Samuel 5); UNC 9 (Williams 3)
Field Goal Pct.: Rhode Island .319; UNC .568
Free Throw Pct.: Rhode Island .636; UNC .733
Three-Point Field Goal Pct.: Rhode Island .333; UNC .429
Three-Point Field Goal Shooting: Rhode Island (Brown 4-9, Samuel 0-2, Cofield 1-6, Easterling 1-1, Fox 0-1, Ivey-Jones 1-1, Keebler 0-1); UNC (Reese 1-2, Williams 3-5, Phelps 1-1, Sullivan 0-1, Calabria 0-1, Davis 0-2, Cherry 1-1, Stephenson 0-1)
Technical Fouls: None
Officials: Garibaldi, Valentine, Grzywinski

NORTH CAROLINA 80
ARKANSAS 74

FRIDAY, MARCH 26, 1993
BRENDAN BYRNE ARENA, EAST RUTHERFORD, N.J.
(ATTENDANCE: 19,761)
SEMIFINAL, NCAA EAST REGIONAL

Arkansas	FG	FT	REB	A	PF	TP
Hawkins	2-10	0-0	4	2	2	5
Thurman	5-12	0-0	0	1	1	12
Stewart	2-3	0-0	1	1	3	5
Beck	0-2	0-0	2	5	4	0
Shepherd	5-8	0-0	3	2	0	13
Linn	0-1	0-0	1	0	0	0
McDaniel	3-12	3-4	6	1	4	12
Crawford	1-2	1-2	3	3	1	4
Williamson	7-7	2-3	2	1	3	16
Martin	2-4	3-4	5	5	2	7
Totals	27-61	9-13	31	21	20	74

North Carolina	FG	FT	REB	A	PF	TP
Reese	5-11	3-6	8	4	1	13
Lynch	9-13	5-7	10	2	4	23
Montross	6-8	3-6	8	1	2	15
Phelps	2-5	0-1	7	7	1	5
Williams	7-19	5-6	1	3	3	22
Sullivan	1-4	0-0	1	2	0	2
Rodl	0-1	0-0	1	2	1	0
Cherry	0-0	0-0	0	0	0	0
Salvadori	0-1	0-0	2	0	1	0
Totals	30-62	16-26	45	19	13	80

Arkansas	45	29	—	74
North Carolina	45	35	—	80

Turnovers: Arkansas 12 (Shepherd 6); UNC 12 (Lynch 3)
Blocked Shots: Arkansas 6 (Williamson, Martin 2); UNC 3 (Montross 2)
Steals: Arkansas 6 (Thurman, Shepherd 2); UNC 5 (Phelps 2)
Field Goal Pct.: Arkansas .443; UNC .484
Free Throw Pct.: Arkansas .692; UNC .615
Three-Point Field Goal Pct.: Arkansas .458; UNC .333
Three-Point Field Goal Shooting: Arkansas (Hawkins 1-4, Thurman 2-5, Stewart 1-1, Shepherd 3-4, Linn 0-1, McDaniel 3-8, Crawford 1-1); UNC (Reese 0-1, Phelps 1-1, Williams 3-9, Rodl 0-1)
Technical Fouls: None
Officials: Hillary, Harrington, Sanzere

HUGH MORTON

The intensity and physical play of the ACC regular season more than prepared the Tar Heels for the postseason.

NORTH CAROLINA 75 / CINCINNATI 68

SUNDAY, MARCH 28, 1993
BRENDAN BYRNE ARENA, EAST RUTHERFORD, N.J.
(ATTENDANCE: 19,761)
FINAL, NCAA EAST REGIONAL

Cincinnati	FG	FT	REB	A	PF	TP
Martin	6-11	4-4	6	2	5	16
Nelson	2-3	0-0	5	2	1	4
Blount	3-10	2-2	9	2	4	8
Gibson	5-11	0-0	5	6	3	13
Van Exel	8-24	1-2	3	5	1	23
Gregor	1-5	0-1	2	1	2	2
Durden	0-2	0-0	0	0	0	0
Harris	0-0	0-0	1	0	0	0
Bostic	1-3	0-0	3	1	5	2
Jacobs	0-1	0-0	0	0	0	0
Totals	26-70	7-9	39	19	21	68

North Carolina	FG	FT	REB	A	PF	TP
Reese	2-9	4-4	3	3	2	8
Lynch	7-14	7-9	14	0	2	21
Montross	6-8	3-6	7	0	4	15
Phelps	0-3	3-4	2	7	2	3
Williams	8-17	1-2	1	0	3	20
Sullivan	2-4	0-0	2	2	0	4
Rodl	1-1	0-0	0	2	1	2
Calabria	0-0	0-0	0	0	0	0
Salvadori	1-2	0-0	5	0	1	2
Totals	27-58	18-25	43	14	15	75

Cincinnati	37	29	2	— 68
North Carolina	36	30	9	— 75

Turnovers: Cincinnati 18 (Gibson 4); UNC 18 (Reese 5)
Blocked Shots: Cincinnati 6 (Martin 2); UNC 5 (Salvadori 2)
Steals: Cincinnati 11 (Van Exel 5); UNC 11 (Lynch 6)
Field Goal Pct.: Cincinnati .371; UNC .466
Free Throw Pct.: Cincinnati .778; UNC .720
Three-Point Field Goal Pct.: Cincinnati .375; UNC .375
Three-Point Field Goal Shooting: Cincinnati (Nelson 0-1, Gibson 3-8, Van Exel 6-13, Durden 0-2); UNC (Reese 0-1, Wiliams 3-7)
Technical Fouls: None
Officials: Silvester, McDonald, Valentine

NORTH CAROLINA 78 / KANSAS 68

SATURDAY, APRIL 3, 1993
LOUISIANA SUPERDOME, NEW ORLEANS, LA.
(ATTENDANCE: 64,151)
NATIONAL SEMIFINAL

Kansas	FG	FT	REB	A	PF	TP
Hancock	2-5	2-2	5	1	1	6
Scott	3-5	2-2	1	1	5	8
Pauley	2-5	1-1	9	2	3	5
Walters	7-15	0-0	0	5	2	19
Jordan	7-13	0-0	1	4	1	19
Rayford	0-0	0-0	0	0	0	0
Woodberry	2-5	0-0	2	2	4	4
Richey	1-4	0-0	2	0	1	2
Ostertag	0-2	2-2	2	0	3	2
Gurley	1-2	0-0	0	0	0	3
Pearson	0-1	0-0	0	0	0	0
Totals	25-57	7-7	24	15	20	68

North Carolina	FG	FT	REB	A	PF	TP
Reese	3-5	1-2	4	6	0	7
Lynch	5-12	4-6	10	0	3	14
Montross	9-14	5-8	4	1	4	23
Phelps	1-3	1-2	5	6	2	3
Williams	7-11	6-6	3	0	1	25
Sullivan	0-2	0-0	1	1	1	0
Rodl	0-0	0-0	0	2	2	0
Salvadori	3-5	0-0	3	1	0	6
Calabria	0-0	0-0	0	0	0	0
Cherry	0-0	0-0	2	0	0	0
Davis	0-0	0-0	0	0	0	0
Stephenson	0-0	0-0	0	0	0	0
Geth	0-0	0-0	0	0	0	0
Wenstrom	0-0	0-0	0	0	0	0
Totals	28-52	17-24	35	17	13	78

Kansas	36	32	— 68
North Carolina	40	38	— 78

Turnovers: Kansas 16 (Walters 6); UNC 16 (Phelps 4)
Blocked Shots: Kansas 4 (Richey 2); UNC 1 (Salvadori)
Steals: Kansas 5 (Hancock, Scott, Walters, Jordan, Ostertag 1); UNC 8 (Lynch, Montross, Phelps 2)
Field Goal Pct.: Kansas .439; UNC .538
Free Throw Pct.: Kansas 1.000; UNC .708
Three-Point Field Goal Pct.: Kansas .550; UNC .714
Three-Point Field Goal Shooting: Kansas (Walters 5-9, Jordan 5-7, Woodberry 0-2, Gurley 1-1, Pearson 0-1); UNC (Williams 5-7)
Technical Fouls: None
Officials: Clougherty, Burr, Valentine

NORTH CAROLINA 77 / MICHIGAN 71

MONDAY, APRIL 5, 1993
LOUISIANA SUPERDOME, NEW ORLEANS, LA.
(ATTENDANCE: 64,151)
NATIONAL FINAL

North Carolina	FG	FT	REB	A	PF	TP
Reese	2-7	4-4	5	3	1	8
Lynch	6-12	0-0	10	1	3	12
Montross	5-11	6-9	5	0	2	16
Phelps	4-6	1-2	3	6	0	9
Williams	8-12	4-4	1	1	1	25
Sullivan	1-2	1-2	1	1	2	3
Salvadori	0-0	2-2	4	1	1	2
Rodl	1-4	0-0	0	0	0	2
Calabria	0-0	0-0	0	0	0	0
Wenstrom	0-1	0-0	0	0	0	0
Cherry	0-0	0-0	0	0	0	0
Totals	27-55	18-23	29	13	10	77

Michigan	FG	FT	REB	A	PF	TP
Webber	11-18	1-2	11	1	2	23
Jackson	2-3	2-2	1	1	5	6
Howard	3-8	1-1	7	3	3	7
Rose	5-12	0-0	1	4	3	12
King	6-13	2-2	6	4	2	15
Riley	1-3	0-0	3	1	1	2
Pelinka	2-4	0-0	2	1	1	6
Talley	0-0	0-0	0	1	1	0
Voskuil	0-1	0-0	0	1	0	0
Totals	30-62	6-7	33	17	18	71

North Carolina	42	35	— 77
Michigan	36	35	— 71

Turnovers: UNC 10 (Phelps 5); Michigan 14 (Rose 6)
Blocked Shots: UNC 4 (Lynch 2); Michigan 4 (Webber 3)
Steals: UNC 7 (Phelps 3); Michigan 4 (Webber, Jackson, King, Riley)
Field Goal Pct.: UNC .491; Michigan .484
Free Throw Pct.: UNC .783; Michigan .857
Three-Point Field Goal Pct.: UNC .455; Michigan .333
Three-Point Field Goal Shooting: UNC (Reese 0-1, Phelps 0-1, Williams 5-7, Rodl 0-2); Michigan (Webber 0-1, Rose 2-6, King 1-5, Pelinka 2-3)
Technical Fouls: Michigan bench (excessive TOs)
Officials: Hightower, Harrington, Stupin

HUGH MORTON

The Tar Heels capped the season with another championship and another New Orleans-style celebration.

REMEMBRANCE OF THINGS PAST
The 1957 Championship

North Carolina (32-0, 14-0 ACC)

DATE	RESULTS		OPPONENTS	SITE
Dec. 4	W	94-66	Furman	H
Dec. 8	W	94-75	Clemson	Charlotte, N.C.
Dec. 12	W	82-55	George Washington	Norfolk, Va.
Dec. 15	W	90-86	South Carolina	A
Dec. 17	W	70-61	Maryland	H
Dec. 20	W	64-59	New York University	New York, N.Y.
Dec. 21	W	89-61	Dartmouth	Boston, Mass.
Dec. 22	W	83-70	Holy Cross	Boston, Mass.
Dec. 27	W	97-76	Utah	Raleigh, N.C.
Dec. 28	W	87-71	Duke	Raleigh, N.C.
Dec. 29	W	63-55	Wake Forest	Raleigh, N.C.
Jan. 8	W	71-61	William & Mary	A
Jan. 11	W	86-54	Clemson	H
Jan. 12	W	102-90	Virginia	H
Jan. 15	W	83-57	N.C. State	A
Jan. 30	W	77-59	Western Carolina	A
Feb. 5	W	*65-61	Maryland	A
Feb. 9	W	75-73	Duke	H
Feb. 11	W	68-59	Virginia	A
Feb. 13	W	72-69	Wake Forest	H
Feb. 19	W	86-57	N.C. State	H
Feb. 22	W	75-62	South Carolina	H
Feb. 26	W	69-64	Wake Forest	A
Mar. 1	W	86-72	Duke	A
Mar. 7	W	81-61	Clemson	Raleigh, N.C.
Mar. 8	W	61-59	Wake Forest	Raleigh, N.C.
Mar. 9	W	95-75	South Carolina	Raleigh, N.C.
Mar. 12	W	90-74	Yale	New York, N.Y.
Mar. 15	W	87-75	Canisius	Philadelphia, Pa.
Mar. 16	W	67-58	Syracuse	Philadelphia, Pa.
Mar. 22	W	**74-70	Michigan State	Kansas City, Mo.
Mar. 23	W	**54-53	Kansas	Kansas City, Mo.

* Two Overtimes
** Three Overtimes

Player	G	FGM	FGA	Pct.	FTM	FTA	Pct.	Reb.	Avg.	PF	Pts.	Avg.
Lennie Rosenbluth	32	305	631	.483	285	376	.758	280	8.8	78	895	28.0
Pete Brennan	32	143	363	.394	185	262	.706	332	10.4	99	471	14.7
Tommy Kearns	32	138	318	.434	135	190	.711	100	3.1	82	411	12.8
Joe Quigg	31	111	256	.434	97	135	.719	268	8.7	89	319	10.3
Bob Cunningham	32	88	224	.393	55	92	.598	214	6.6	111	231	7.2
Tony Radovich	16	21	40	.525	20	26	.769	29	1.8	27	62	3.9
Bill Hathaway	15	16	48	.333	10	24	.416	75	5.0	10	42	2.8
Stan Groll	12	10	27	.370	5	9	.556	18	1.5	10	25	2.1
Bob Young	15	11	43	.256	7	13	.538	32	2.1	32	29	1.9
Ken Rosemond	15	6	15	.400	5	9	.556	9	0.6	9	17	1.1
Danny Lotz	24	7	20	.350	9	23	.391	39	1.6	29	23	0.9
Gehrmann Holland	12	4	8	.500	0	1	.000	6	0.5	5	8	0.7
Roy Searcy	11	0	3	.000	4	5	.800	11	1.0	5	4	0.4
North Carolina	32	860	1996	.431	817	1165	.701	1495	46.7	586	2537	79.3
Opponents	32	720	2043	.352	658	956	.688	1151	35.9	761	2098	65.5

NORTH CAROLINA 74
MICHIGAN STATE 70

MARCH 22, 1957
MUNICIPAL AUDITORIUM, KANSAS CITY, MO.
(ATTENDANCE: 10,500)
NATIONAL SEMIFINAL

North Carolina	FG	FT	R	PF	TP
Rosenbluth	11-42	7-9	3	1	29
Cunningham	9-18	3-5	12	5	21
Brennan	6-16	2-4	17	5	14
Kearns	1-8	4-5	6	4	6
Quigg	0-1	2-3	4	5	2
Lotz	0-1	0-0	4	1	0
Young	1-3	0-1	2	1	2
Searcy	0-0	0-0	1	0	0
Totals	28-89	18-27	54	22	74

Michigan State	FG	FT	R	PF	TP
Quiggle	6-21	8-10	10	1	20
Green	4-12	3-6	19	2	11
Ferguson	4-8	2-3	1	5	10
Hedden	4-20	6-7	15	5	14
Wilson	0-3	2-2	5	1	2
Anderregg	2-7	3-6	3	2	7
Bencie	1-6	0-0	2	1	2
Scott	2-3	0-2	3	1	4
Totals	23-80	24-36	65	18	70

North Carolina	29	29	6	2	8	— 74
Michigan	29	29	6	2	4	— 70

NORTH CAROLINA 54
KANSAS 53

MARCH 23, 1957
MUNICIPAL AUDITORIUM, KANSAS CITY, MO.
(ATTENDANCE: 10,500)
NATIONAL SEMIFINAL

North Carolina	FG	FT	R	PF	TP
Rosenbluth	8-15	4-4	5	5	20
Cunningham	0-3	0-1	5	4	0
Brennan	4-8	3-7	11	3	11
Kearns	4-8	3-7	1	4	11
Quigg	4-10	2-3	9	4	10
Lotz	0-0	0-0	2	0	0
Young	1-1	0-0	3	1	2
Totals	21-45	12-22	42	21	54

Kansas	FG	FT	R	PF	TP
Chamberlain	6-13	11-16	14	3	23
King	3-12	5-6	4	4	11
Elstun	4-12	3-6	4	2	11
Parker	2-4	0-0	0	0	4
Loneski	0-5	2-3	3	2	2
L. Johnson	0-1	2-2	0	1	2
Billings	0-0	0-0	0	2	0
Totals	15-47	23-33	28	14	53

North Carolina	29	17	2	0	6	— 54
Michigan	22	24	2	0	5	— 53

"The strongest memory I have of the whole thing is Joe [Quigg] hitting those free throws. He carried the greatest pressure of all and lived the dream of anyone who has ever played basketball by simply making the shots."

Lennie Rosenbluth

REMEMBRANCE OF THINGS PAST
The 1982 Championship

North Carolina (32-2, 12-2 ACC)

DATE	RESULTS		OPPONENTS	SITE
Nov. 28	W	74-67	Kansas	Charlotte, N.C.
Nov. 30	W	73-62	Southern California	Greensboro, N.C.
Dec. 3	W	78-70	Tulsa	H
Dec. 12	W	75-39	South Florida	H
Dec. 19	W	59-36	Rutgers	New York, N.Y.
Dec. 26	W	82-69	Kentucky	East Rutherford, N.J.
Dec. 28	W	*56-50	Penn State	Santa Clara, Calif.
Dec. 29	W	76-57	Santa Clara	Santa Clara, Calif.
Jan. 4	W	64-40	William & Mary	H
Jan. 6	W	66-50	Maryland	A
Jan. 9	W	65-60	Virginia	H
Jan. 13	W	61-41	N.C. State	A
Jan. 16	W	73-63	Duke	A
Jan. 21	L	48-55	Wake Forest	H
Jan. 23	W	66-54	Georgia Tech	A
Jan. 27	W	77-72	Clemson	H
Jan. 30	W	58-44	N.C. State	H
Feb. 3	L	58-74	Virginia	A
Feb. 5	W	96-69	Furman	Charlotte, N.C.
Feb. 6	W	67-46	The Citadel	Charlotte, N.C.
Feb. 11	W	59-56	Maryland	H
Feb. 14	W	66-57	Georgia	Greensboro, N.C.
Feb. 17	W	69-51	Wake Forest	A
Feb. 20	W	55-49	Clemson	A
Feb. 24	W	77-54	Georgia Tech	H
Feb. 27	W	84-66	Duke	H
Mar. 5	W	55-39	Georgia Tech	Greensboro, N.C.
Mar. 6	W	58-46	N.C. State	Greensboro, N.C.
Mar. 7	W	47-45	Virginia	Greensboro, N.C.
Mar. 13	W	52-50	James Madison	Charlotte, N.C.
Mar. 19	W	74-69	Alabama	Raleigh, N.C.
Mar. 21	W	70-60	Villanova	Raleigh, N.C.
Mar. 27	W	68-63	Houston	New Orleans, La.
Mar. 29	W	63-62	Georgetown	New Orleans, La.

* Overtime

Player	G	FGM	FGA	Pct.	FTM	FTA	Pct.	Reb.	Avg.	PF	Pts.	Avg.
James Worthy	34	203	354	.573	126	187	67.4	215	6.3	75	532	15.6
Sam Perkins	32	174	301	.578	109	142	.768	250	7.8	74	457	14.3
Michael Jordan	34	191	358	.534	78	108	.722	149	4.4	91	460	13.5
Matt Doherty	34	122	235	.519	71	92	.772	103	3.0	60	315	9.3
Jimmy Black	34	100	195	.513	59	80	.738	59	1.7	81	259	7.6
Jimmy Braddock	34	28	62	.452	10	12	.833	17	0.5	16	66	1.9
Chris Brust	33	23	37	.622	10	22	.455	56	1.7	17	56	1.7
Buzz Peterson	30	16	41	.390	3	7	.429	14	0.5	10	35	1.2
Cecil Exum	17	8	21	.381	3	11	.273	17	1.0	9	19	1.1
Lynwood Robinson	14	7	11	.636	1	5	.200	3	0.2	1	15	1.1
Jeb Barlow	28	12	31	.387	4	9	.444	23	0.8	17	28	1.0
Warren Martin	19	7	15	.467	0	5	.000	16	0.8	7	14	0.7
John Brownlee	13	4	7	.571	1	5	.200	14	1.1	6	9	0.7
Timo Makkonen	12	0	0	.000	2	4	.500	4	0.3	7	2	0.2
Team								59				
North Carolina	34	895	1668	.537	477	689	.692	999	29.4	.471	*2269	66.7
Opponents	34	811	1742	..466	263	407	.646	873	25.7	641	1885	55.4

* Two of North Carolina's points were scored by a Georgia Tech player.

Deadball Rebounds: North Carolina 88, Opponents 100
Blocked Shots: Perkins 53, Worthy 37, Jordan 8, Black 8, Martin 2, Barlow 1, Brownlee 1
Assists: Black 213, Doherty 105, Worthy 82, Jordan 61, 0Braddock 40, Perkins 35, Peterson 16, Brust 14, Barlow 6, Exum 6, Robinson 3, Martin 1, Makkonen 1
Turnovers: Worthy 94, Black 87, Doherty 64, Jordan 57, Perkins 53, Braddock 23, Brust, 18, Barlow 12, Exum 7, Robinson 6, Brownlee 6, Martin 5, Peterson 4, Makkonen 2
Steals: Black 58, Worthy 52, Jordan 41, Perkins 33, Doherty 26, Brust 8, Braddock 6, Barlow 4, Perterson 4, Robinson 4, Brownlee 1, Exum 1, Martin 1
Fouled Out: Black 4, Jordan 1, Worthy 1

NORTH CAROLINA 68
HOUSTON 63

MARCH 27, 1982
LOUISIANA SUPERDOME, NEW ORLEANS, LA.
(ATTENDANCE: 61,612)
NATIONAL SEMIFINAL

Houston	FG	FT	R	A	TP
Drexler	6-12	5-6	9	3	17
Young	1-7	0-1	3	1	2
Micheaux	8-14	2-3	6	0	18
Rose	10-15	0-2	2	3	20
R. Williams	0-8	2-2	1	2	2
D. Williams	1-3	0-0	1	0	2
Olajuwon	1-3	0-0	6	0	2
Davis	1-2	0-0	0	0	2
Anders	0-2	0-0	0	0	0
Totals	**27-64**	**9-14**	**33**	**9**	**63**

North Carolina	FG	FT	R	A	TP
Doherty	2-7	1-2	1	5	5
Worthy	7-10	0-0	4	3	14
Perkins	9-11	7-7	10	1	25
Black	1-2	4-6	3	4	6
Jordan	7-14	4-4	5	2	18
Peterson	0-0	0-0	1	0	0
Brust	0-0	0-0	0	0	0
Martin	0-0	0-0	0	0	0
Braddock	0-0	0-0	0	0	0
Totals	**26-44**	**16-19**	**26**	**15**	**68**

Houston	29	34	—	63
North Carolina	31	37	—	68

Turnovers: Houston 12, North Carolina 15
Total Fouls: Houston 19, North Carolina 14
Officials: Dabrow, Dibbler, Nichols

NORTH CAROLINA 63
GEORGETOWN 62

MARCH 29, 1982
LOUISIANA SUPERDOME, NEW ORLEANS, LA.
(ATTENDANCE: 61,612)
NATIONAL FINAL

Georgetown	FG	FT	R	A	TP
E. Smith	6-8	2-2	3	5	14
Hancock	0-2	0-0	0	0	0
Ewing	10-15	3-3	11	1	23
Brown	1-2	2-2	2	5	4
Floyd	9-17	0-0	3	5	18
Spriggs	0-2	1-2	1	0	1
Jones	1-3	0-0	0	0	2
Martin	0-2	0-0	0	0	0
G. Smith	0-0	0-0	0	0	0
Totals	**27-51**	**8-9**	**22**	**16**	**62**

North Carolina	FG	FT	R	A	TP
Doherty	1-3	2-3	3	1	4
Worthy	13-17	2-7	4	0	28
Perkins	3-7	4-6	7	1	10
Black	1-4	2-2	3	7	4
Jordan	7-13	2-2	9	2	16
Peterson	0-3	0-0	1	1	0
Braddock	0-0	0-0	0	1	0
Brust	0-0	1-2	1	1	1
Braddock	0-0	0-0	0	0	0
Totals	**25-47**	**13-22**	**30**	**14**	**63**

Georgetown	32	30	—	62
North Carolina	31	32	—	63

Turnovers: Georgetown 12, North Carolina 13
Total Fouls: Georgetown 20, North Carolina 11
Officials: Nichols, Dibbler, Dabrow